I0901147

A Kind of Touching Beauty

A Kind of Touching Beauty

PHOTOGRAPHS OF AMERICA BY **PEDRO MEYER**

TEXT BY **JEAN-PAUL SARTRE**

Seagull
BOOKS

London New York Calcutta

Seagull Books, 2018

First published by Seagull Books, 2012

ISBN 978 0 8574 2 584 3

British Library Cataloguing-in-Publication Data
A catalogue record for this book is available
from the British Library

Jacket and book designed by Sunandini Banerjee, Seagull Books
Printed and bound by Hyam Enterprises, Calcutta

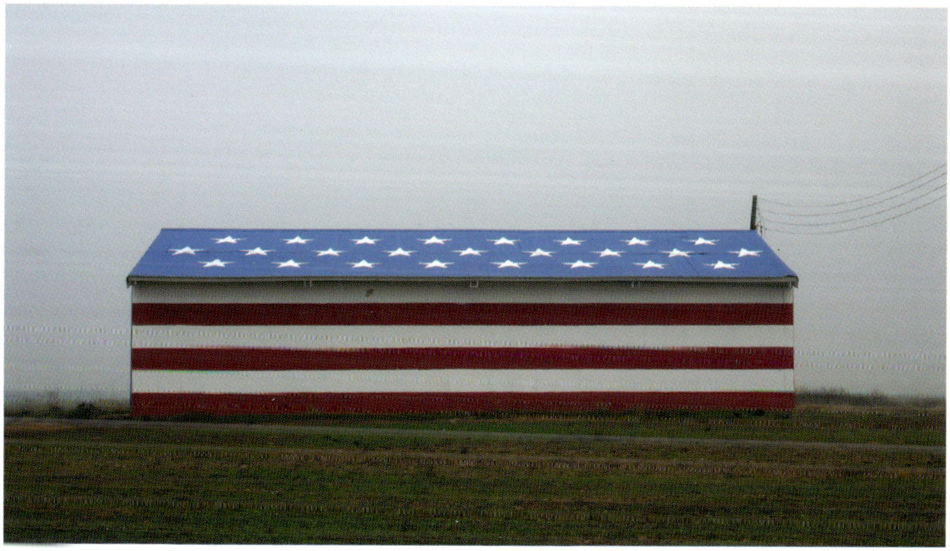

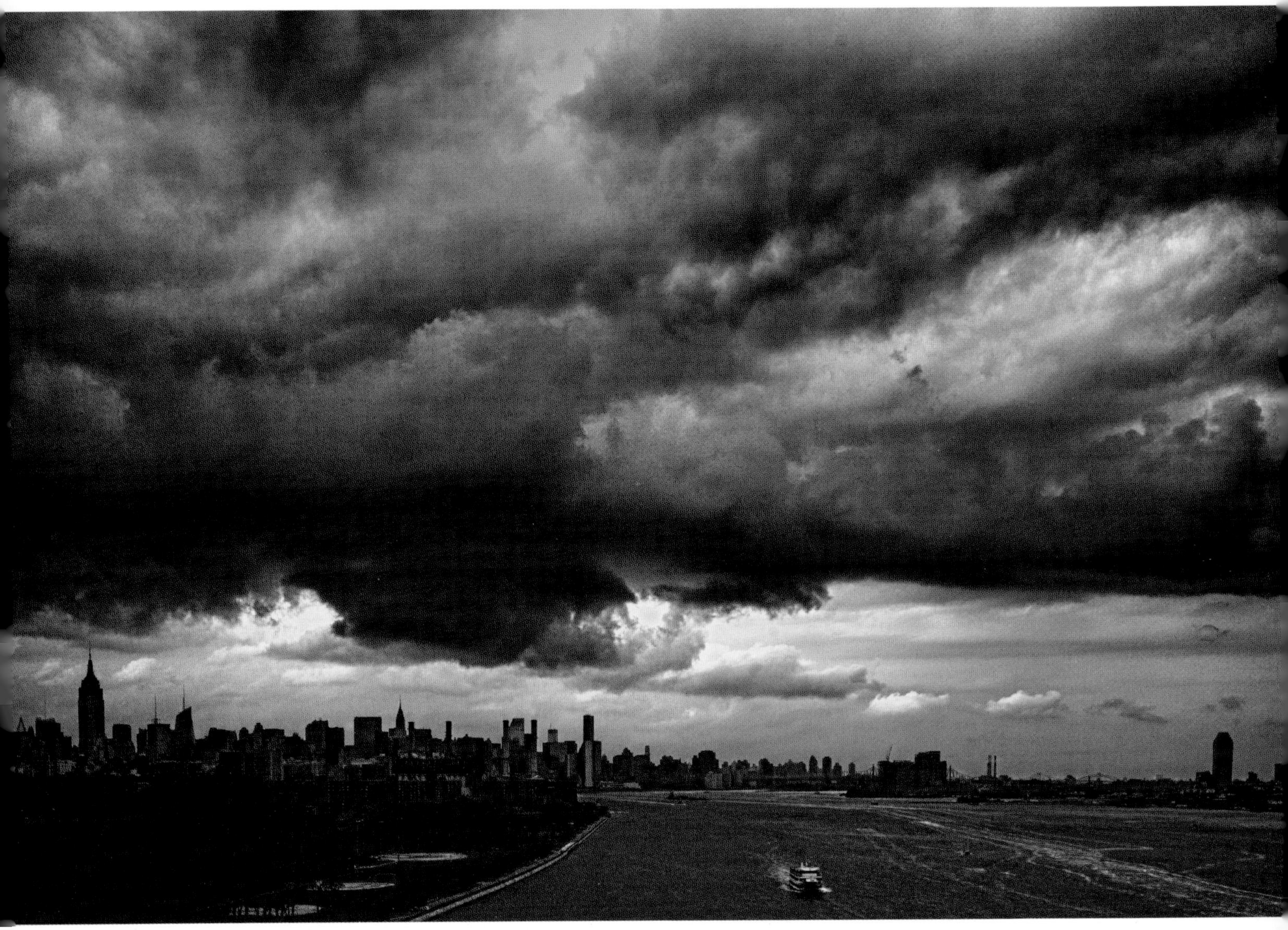

Everyone is free here, not to criticize or to reform how things are done,
but to flee from it and go off into the desert or to some other town.

The cities are open. They are open to the world and to the future.

That is what gives them all an air of adventure;
and, in their disorder and even ugliness,
a kind of touching beauty.

Jean-Paul Sartre, 'Cities of America'

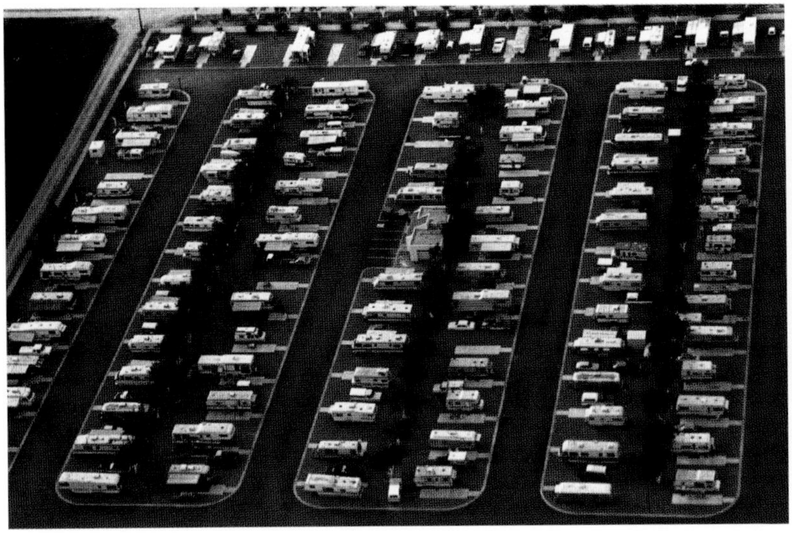

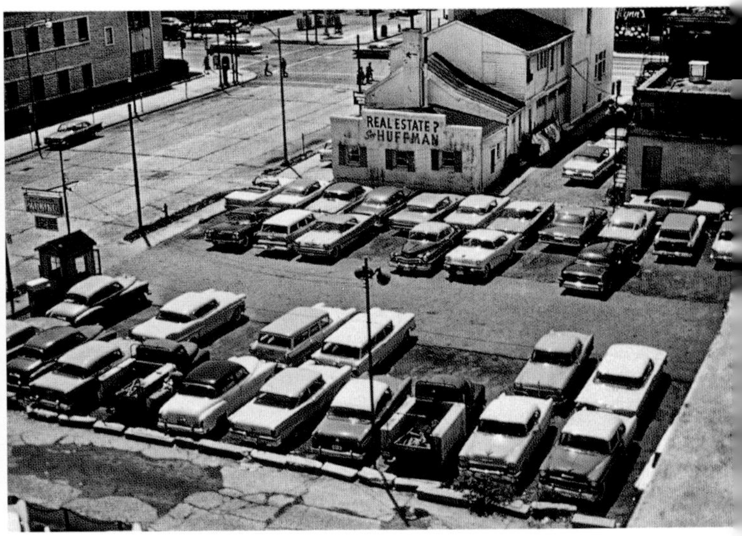
REAL ESTATE?
See HUFFMAN

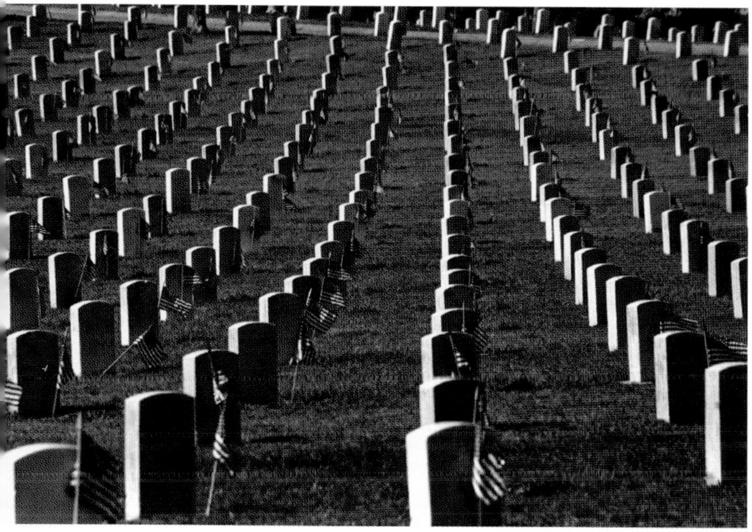

How can you talk about a hundred and thirty-five million Americans?

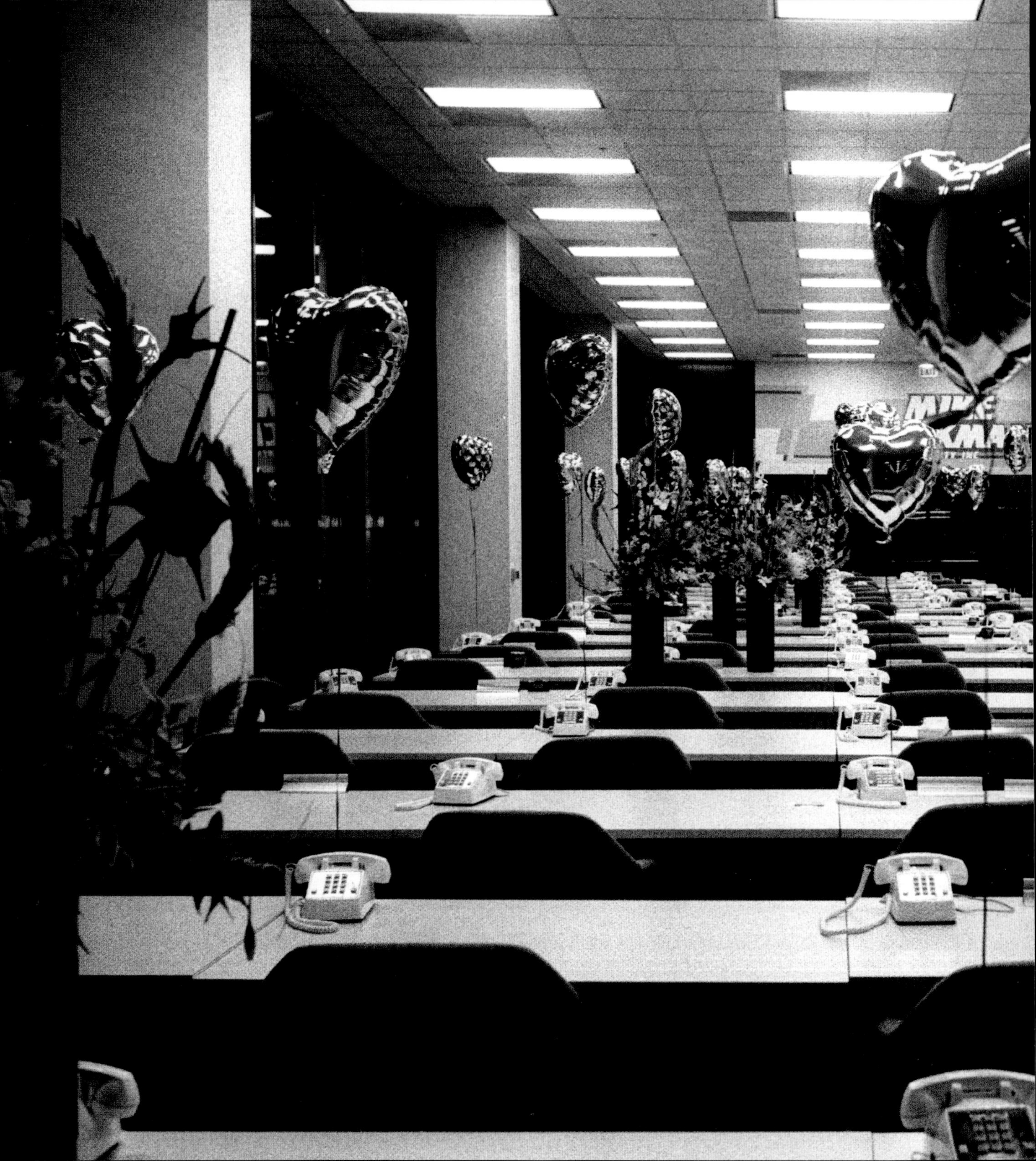

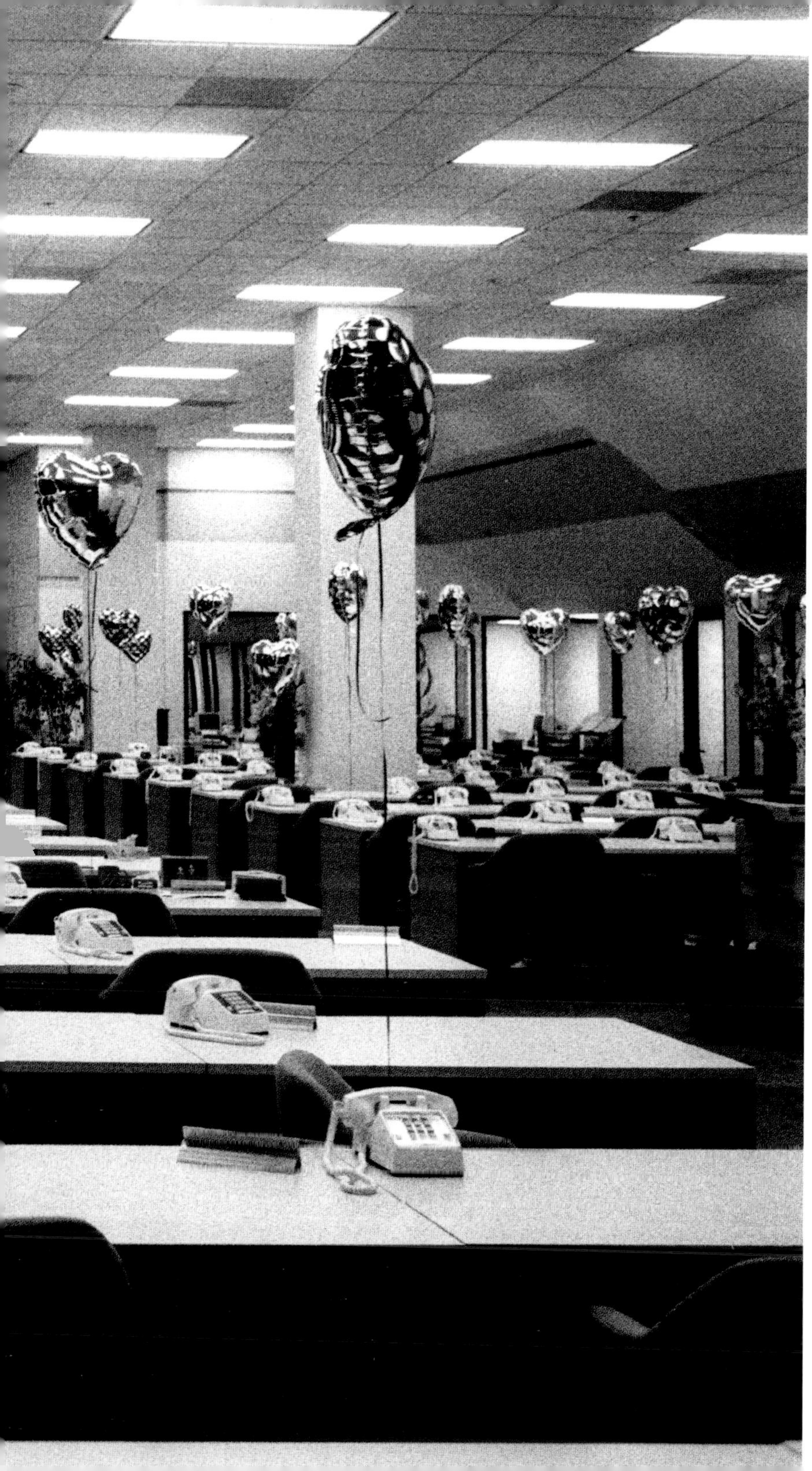

We would need to have lived in this country for ten years and we shall be spending only six weeks here. We are put down in cities where we pick up a few details—yesterday Baltimore, today Knoxville, the day after tomorrow New Orleans—

and then, after admiring the biggest factory or the biggest bridge or the biggest dam in the world,

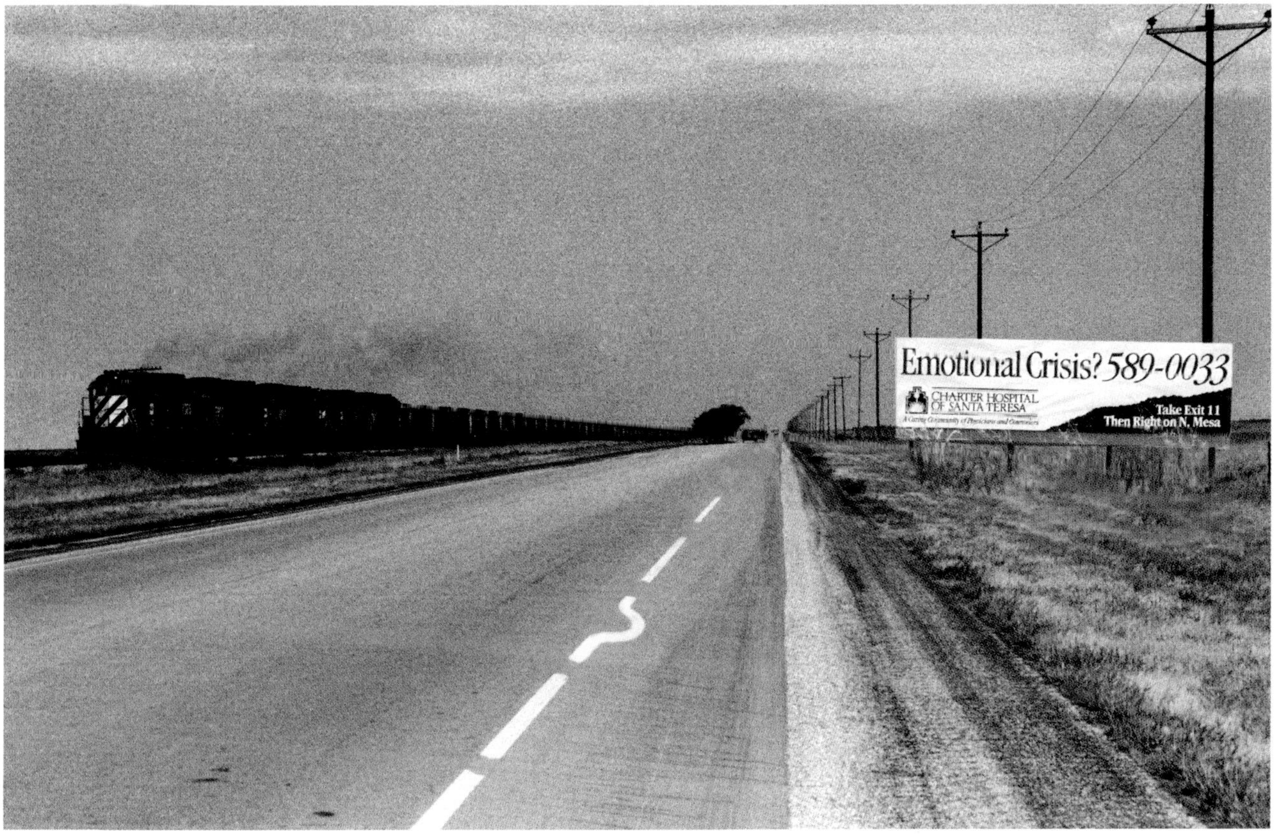
Emotional Crisis? 589-0033
CHARTER HOSPITAL
OF SANTA TERESA
A Caring Community of Physicians and Counselors
Take Exit 11
Then Right on N. Mesa

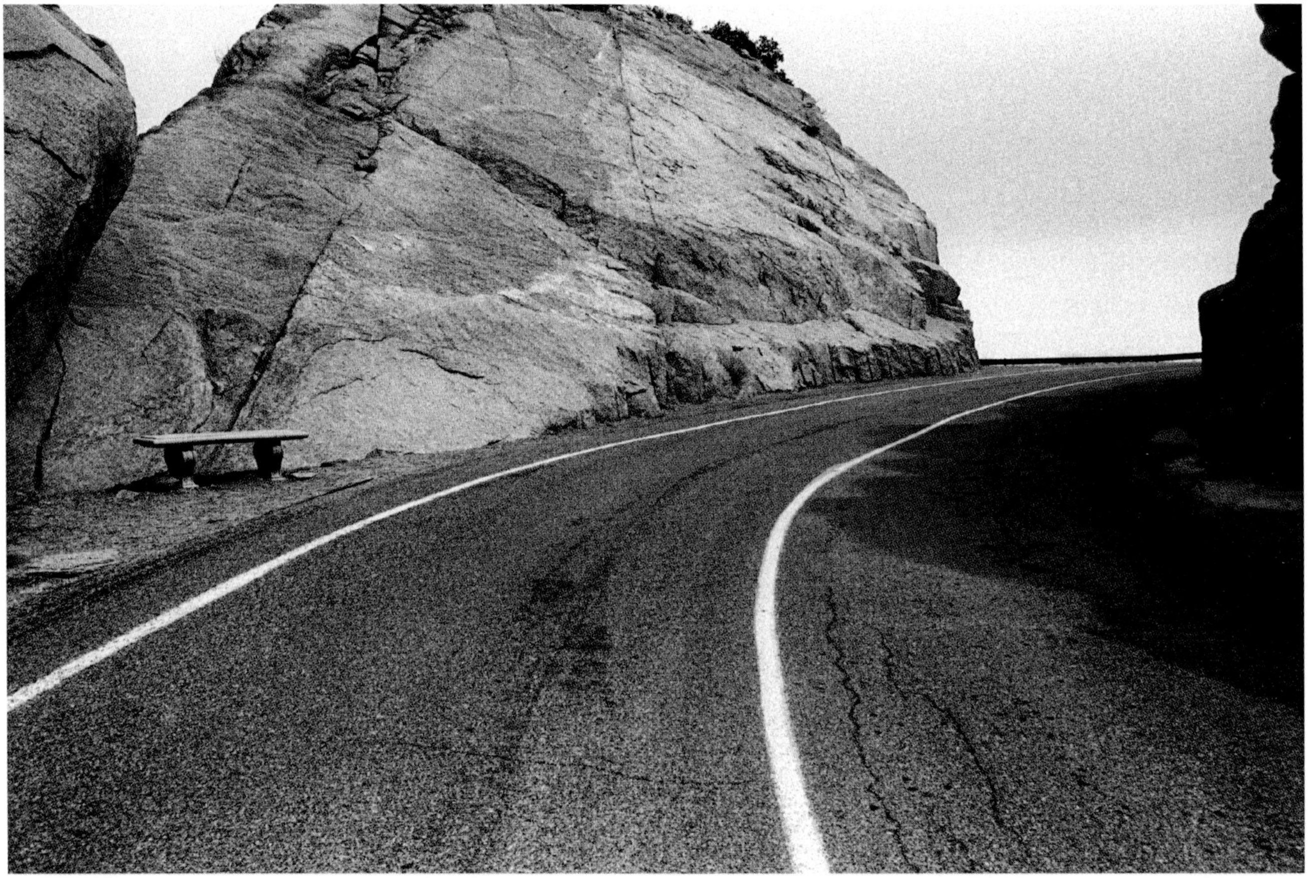

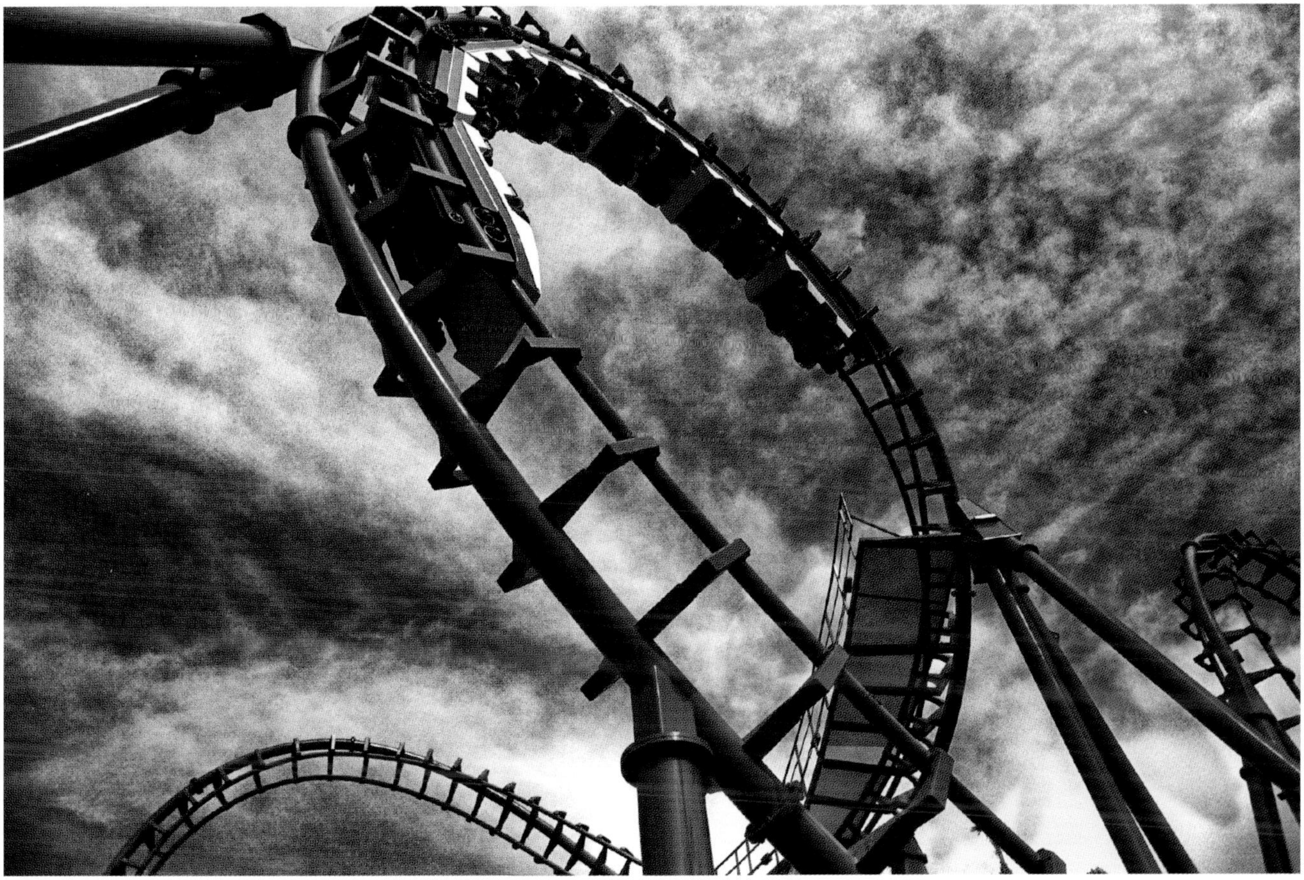

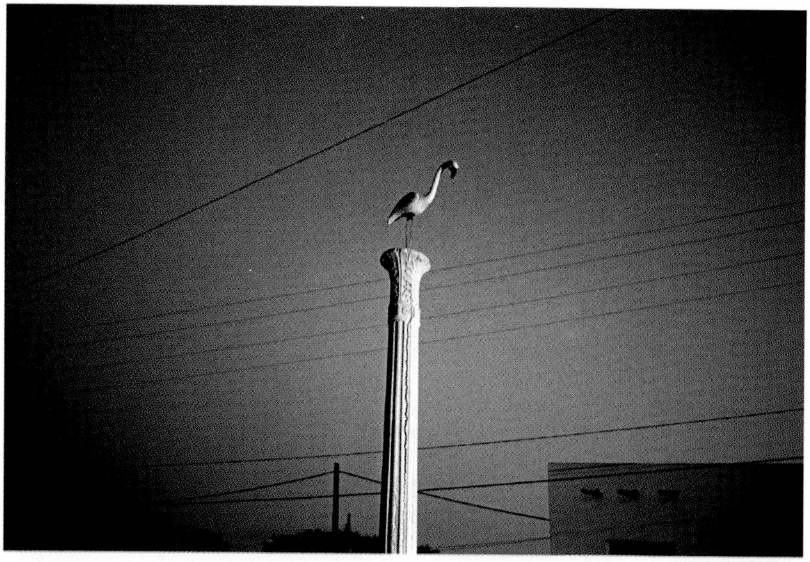

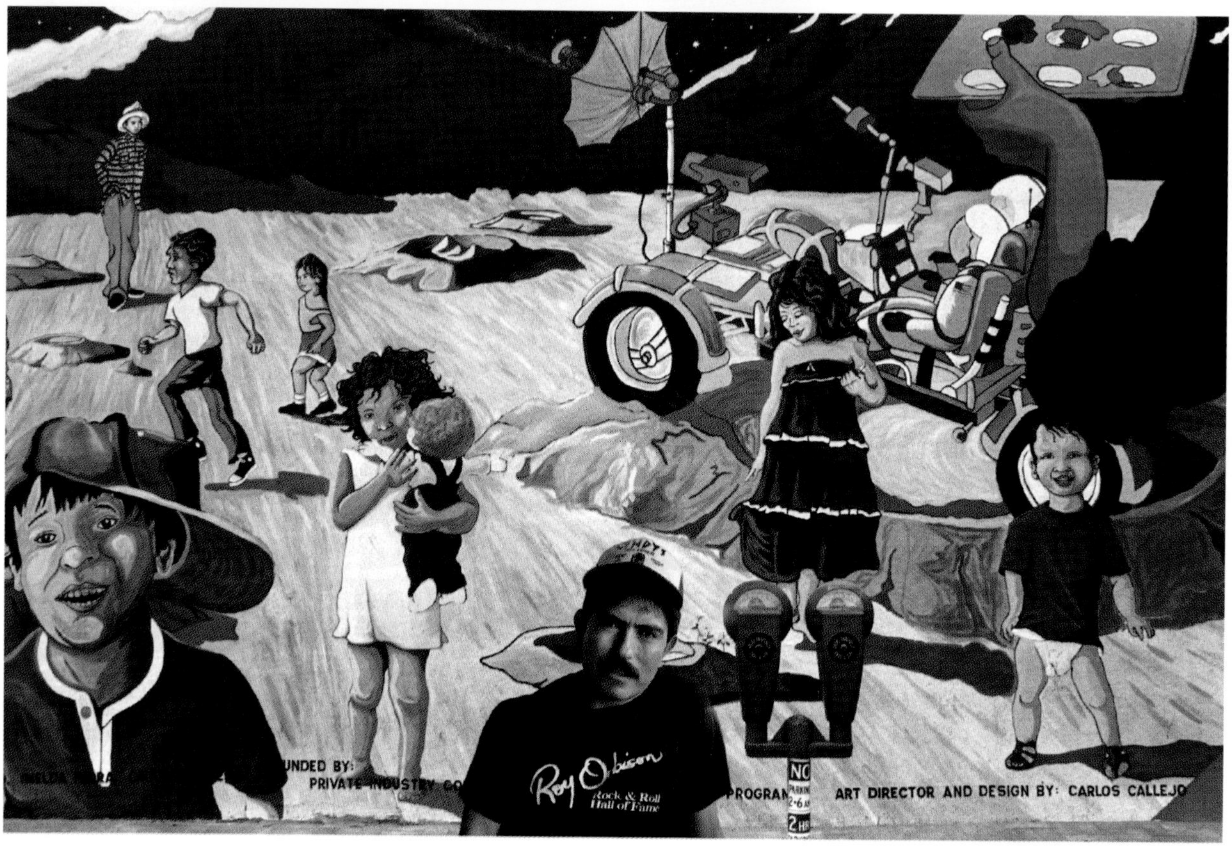
UNDED BY:
PRIVATE INDUSTRY CO
PROGRAM
ART DIRECTOR AND DESIGN BY: CARLOS CALLEJO
Rock & Roll
Hall of Fame
NO
PARKING
2HR

we fly off again, our heads full of facts and figures.

We shall have seen more steel and aluminium than human beings. But can one speak about steel? As for 'impressions', they come as and when they please.

Some say, 'Keep to the facts!'

But what facts? The length of this shipyard in feet or the electric blue of the oxyhydrogen torch in the pale light of this shed? In choosing, I am already deciding what America is.

Others, by contrast, say, 'Step back and get some perspective on things!' But I distrust those perspectives that are already generalizations. So I've decided to convey my personal impressions and constructions, taking the responsibility on myself.

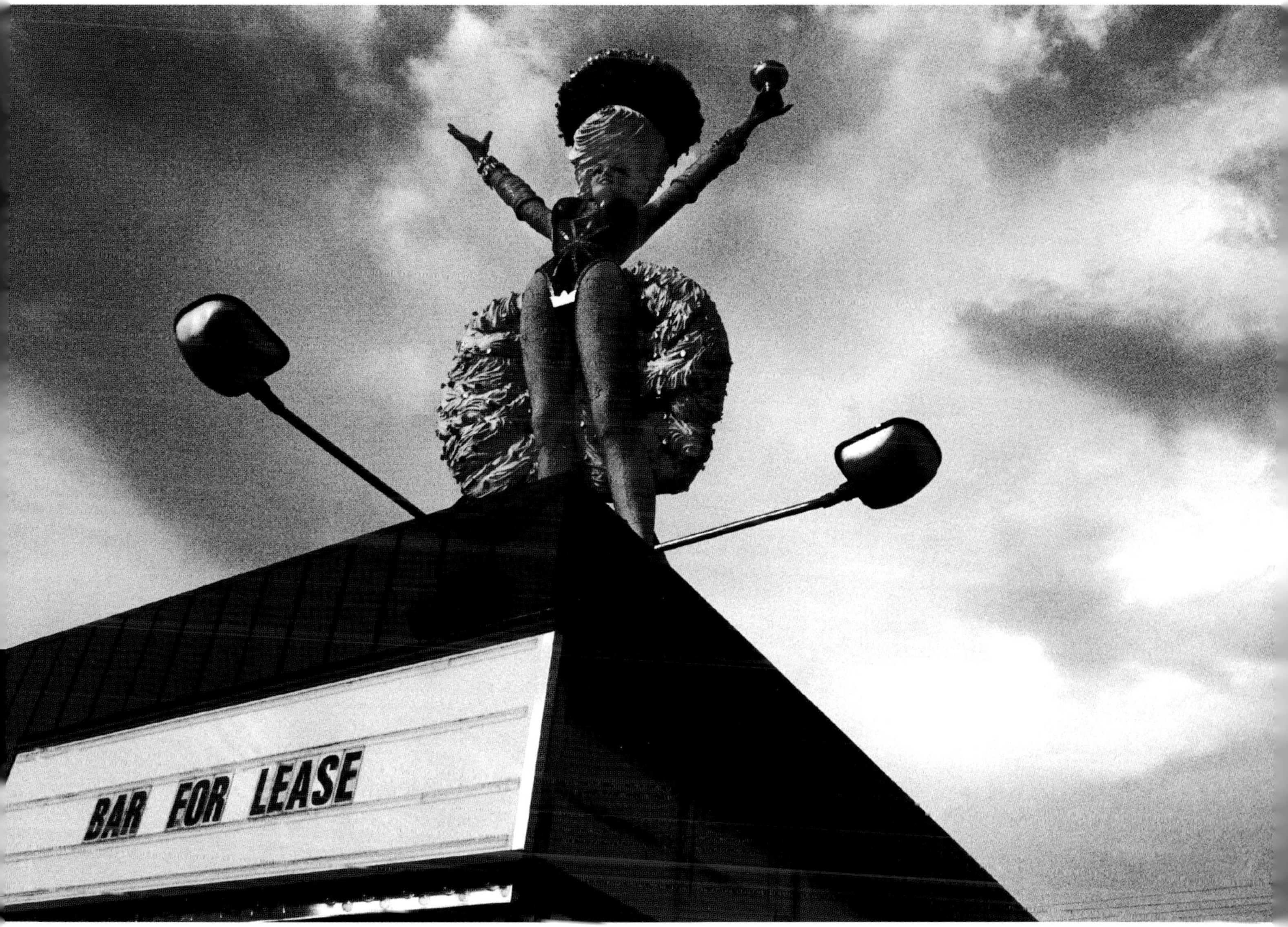
BAR FOR LEASE

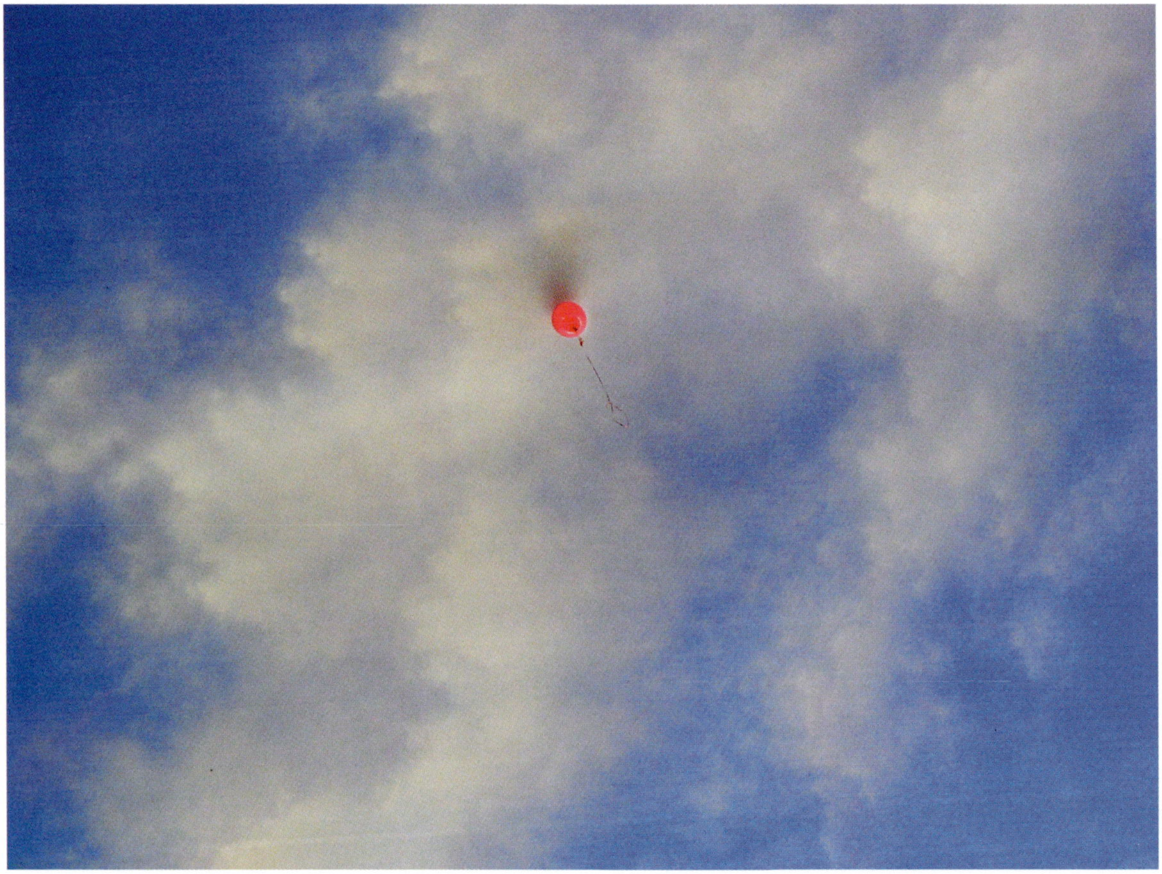

Perhaps I’ve dreamed this America.

I shall, at any rate, be honest with my dream: I shall set it out just as I dreamed it.

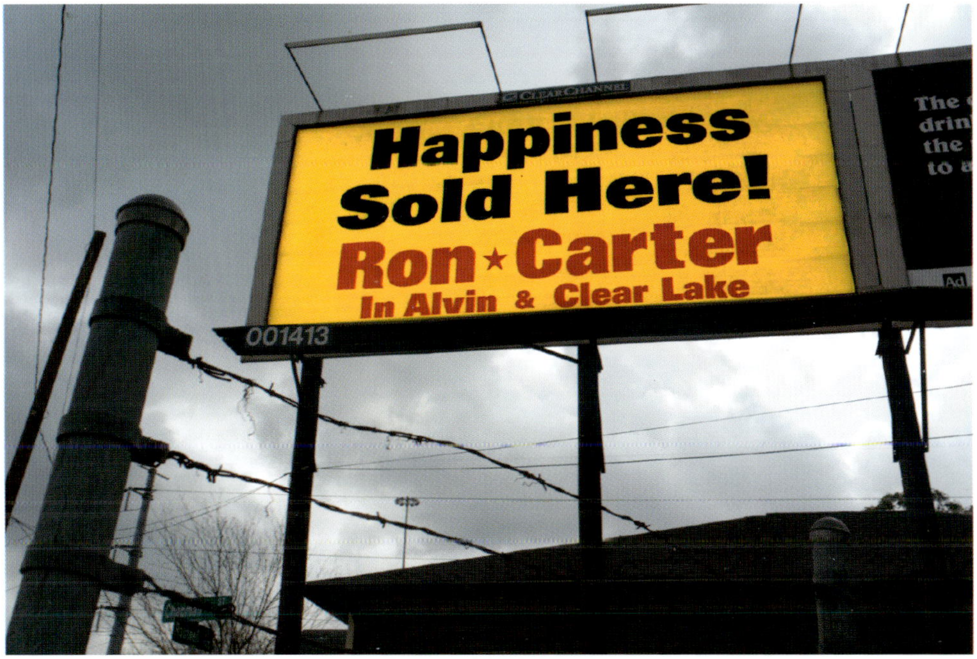
Happiness
Sold Here!
Ron★Carter
In Alvin & Clear Lake
001413

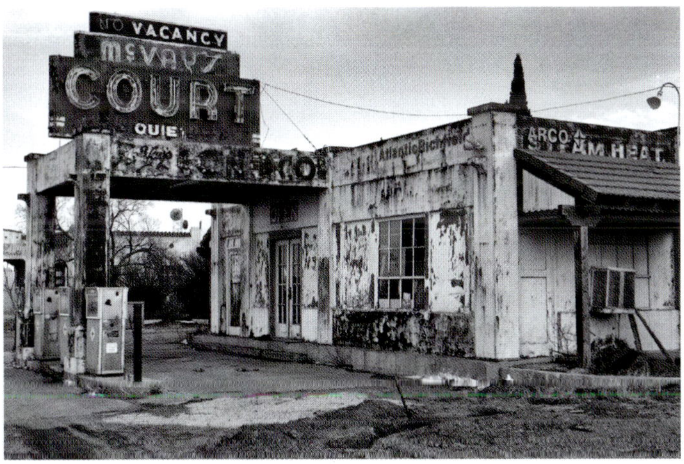
NO VACANCY
COURT
ARCO

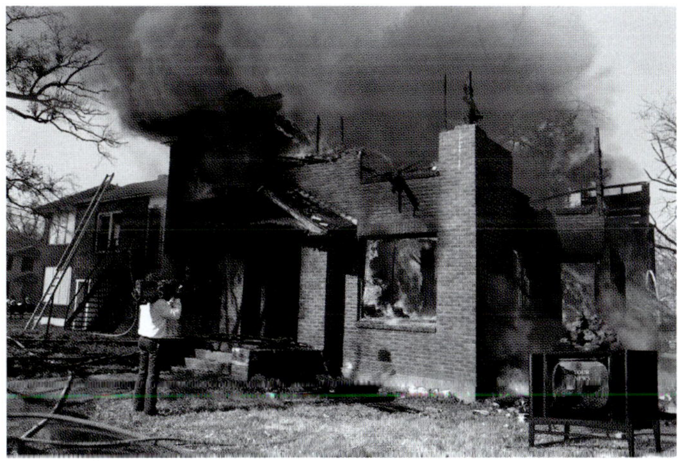

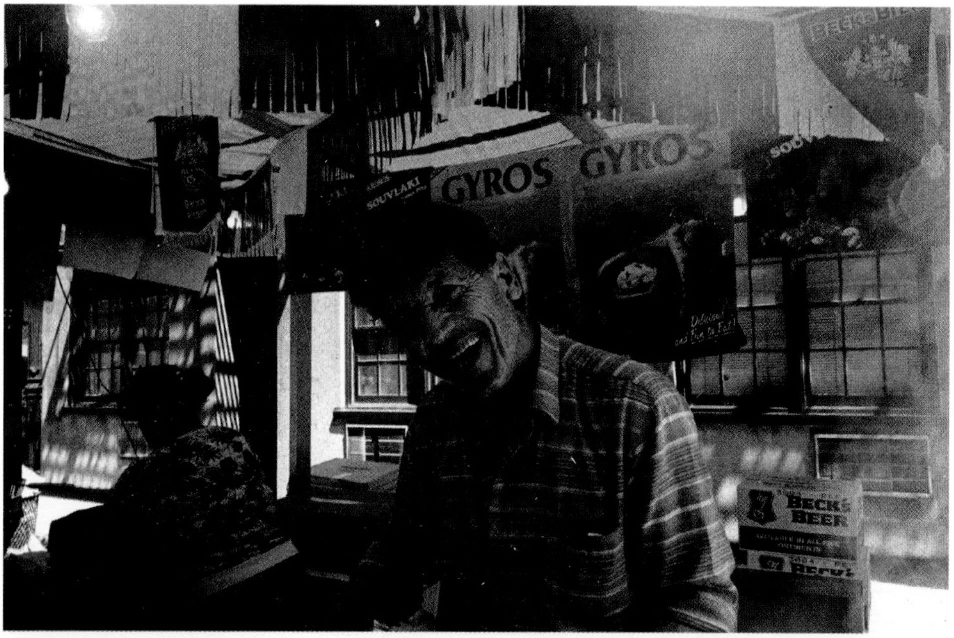
SOUVLAKI
GYROS
GYROS
BECK'S
BEER

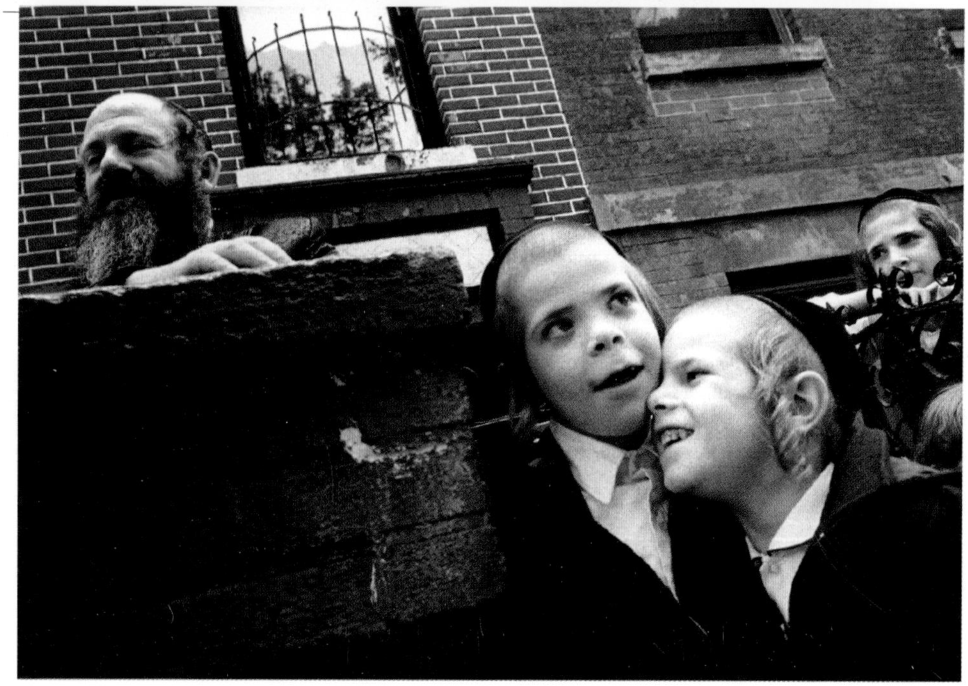

And today I would like to give you my impression of those two contradictory 'slogans' doing the rounds in Paris: 'the American is a conformist' and 'the American is an individualist'.

Like everyone else, I had heard tell of the famous American 'melting pot' which, at various critical temperatures, transforms a Pole, an Italian and a Finn into citizens of the United States. But I did not quite know what it meant.

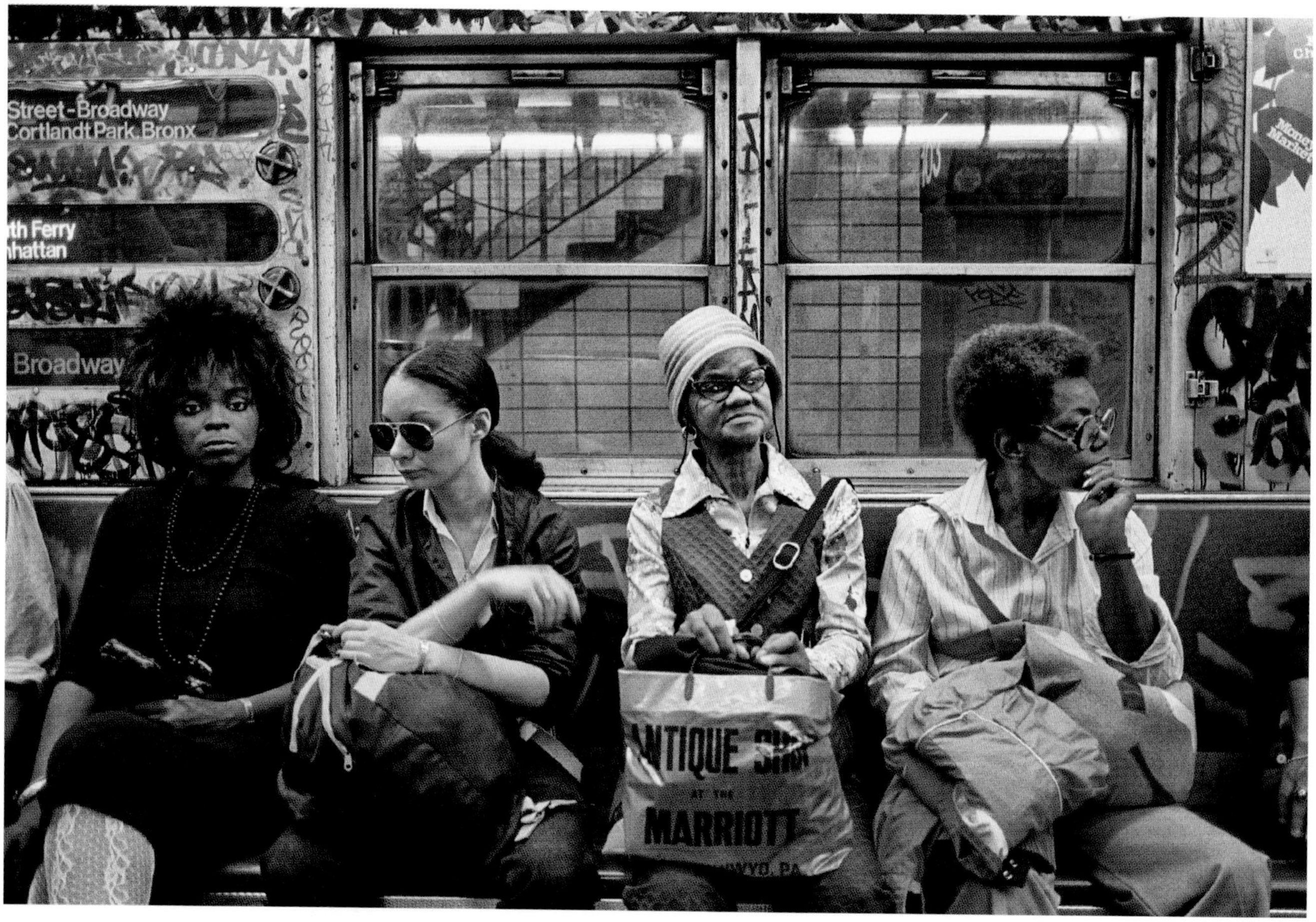
Street-Broadway
Cortlandt Park, Bronx
Broadway
AT THE
MARRIOTT

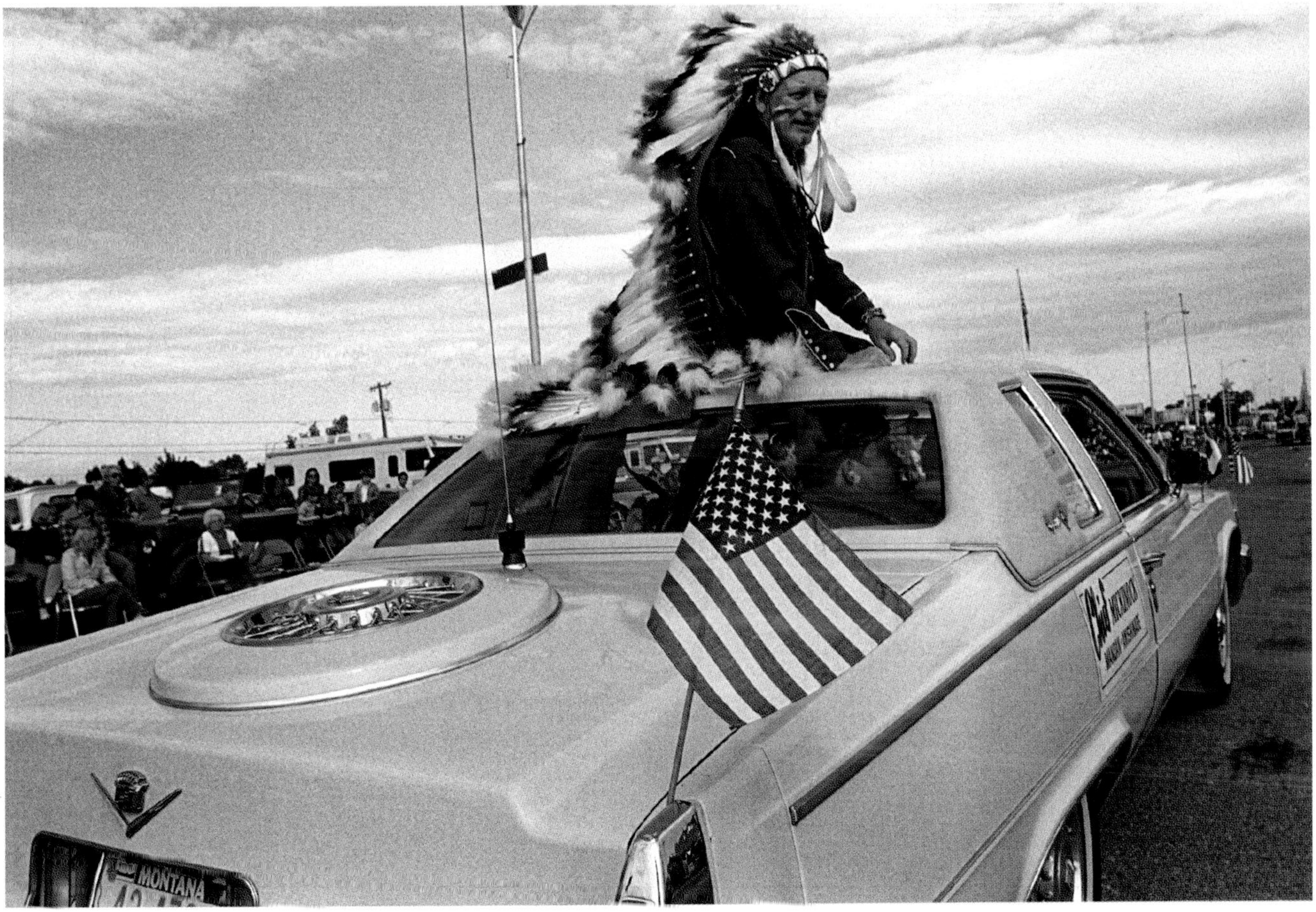
MONTANA

Well, on the very day after I arrived I met a European in the process of 'melting'. In the main lobby of the Plaza Hotel I was introduced to a dark-haired man of quite modest stature who, like everyone here, talked with a slightly nasal twang, without visible movement of his lips or cheeks, who laughed with his mouth, but not with his eyes, and who expressed himself in a good, but heavily accented French, his speech sprinkled with barbarisms and Americanisms.

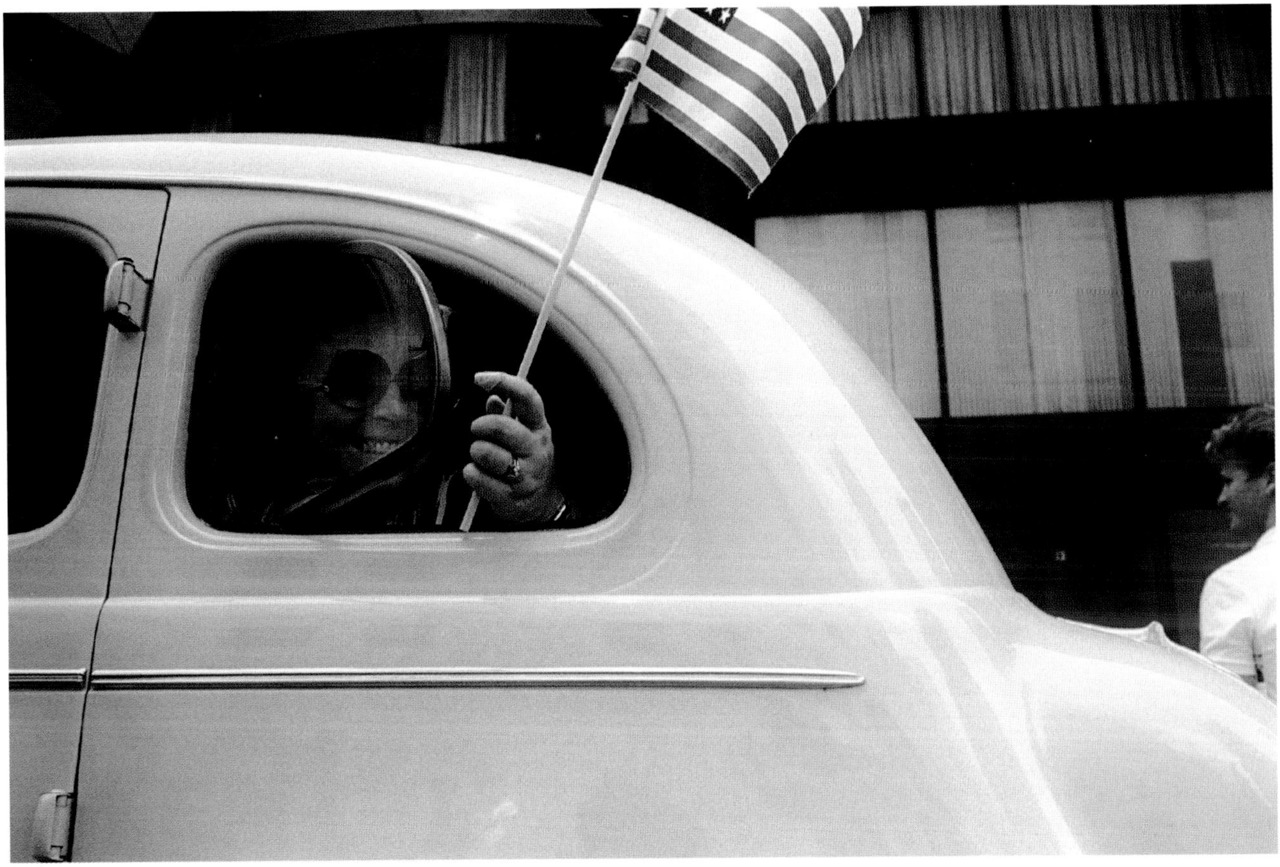

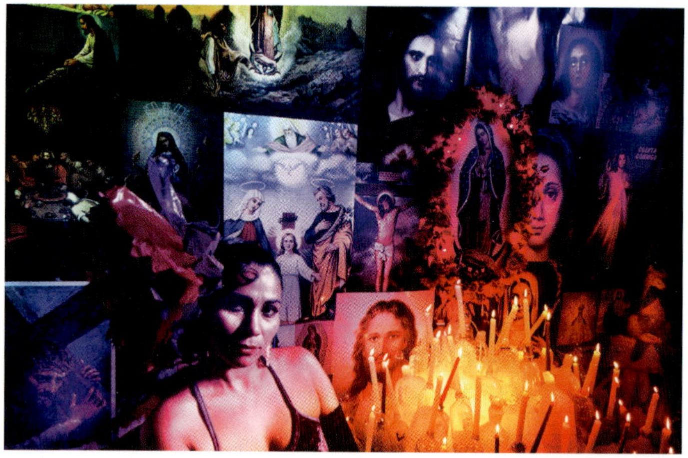

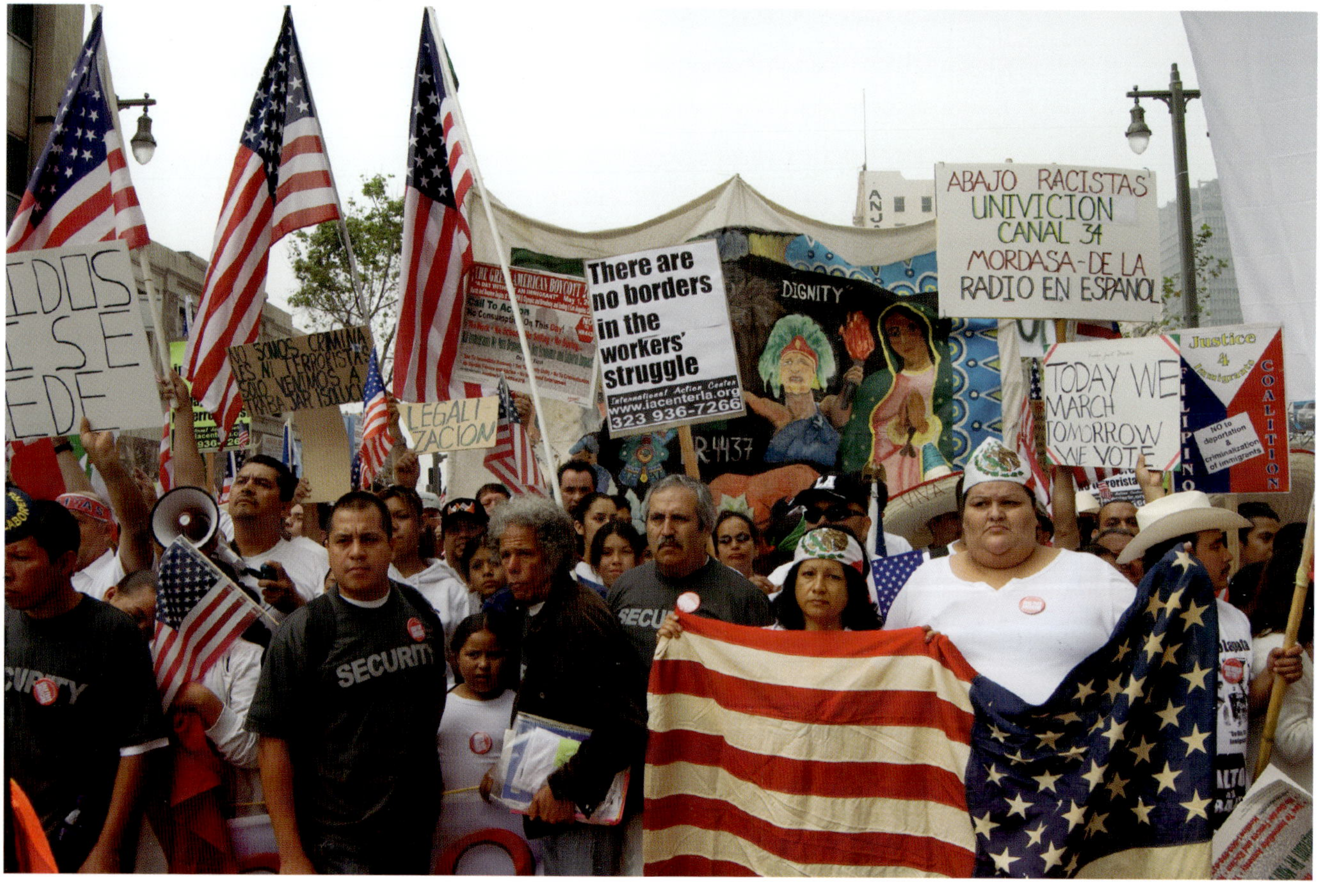

ABAJO RACISTAS
UNIVICION
CANAL 34
MORDASA-DE LA
RADIO EN ESPAÑOL
There are no borders in the workers' struggle
International Action Center
www.iacenterla.org
323 936-7266
DIGNITY
TODAY WE MARCH TOMORROW WE VOTE
Justice 4 Immigrants
FILIPINO
COALITION
NO to deportation & criminalization of immigrants
LEGALI ZACION
SECURITY

When I complimented him on his knowledge of our language, he replied with astonishment, 'But that's because I'm French.' He was born in Paris, has been living in American for only fifteen years and, before the war, went back to France every six months. Yet he is already half in the grip of America. His mother has never left Paris: when he speaks of Paname in deliberately vulgar tones he sounds much more like a Yankee wanting to show off his knowledge of Europe than an exiled Frenchman recalling his homeland. He feels obliged from time to time to cast roguish winks in my direction, saying 'Aha! New Orleans, fine women!' But, in so doing, he is conforming more to the American's idea of the Frenchman than seeking collusion with a compatriot. 'Fine women', and he laughs, but in a forced way.

Puritanism isn't far off and I feel a chill run down my spine.

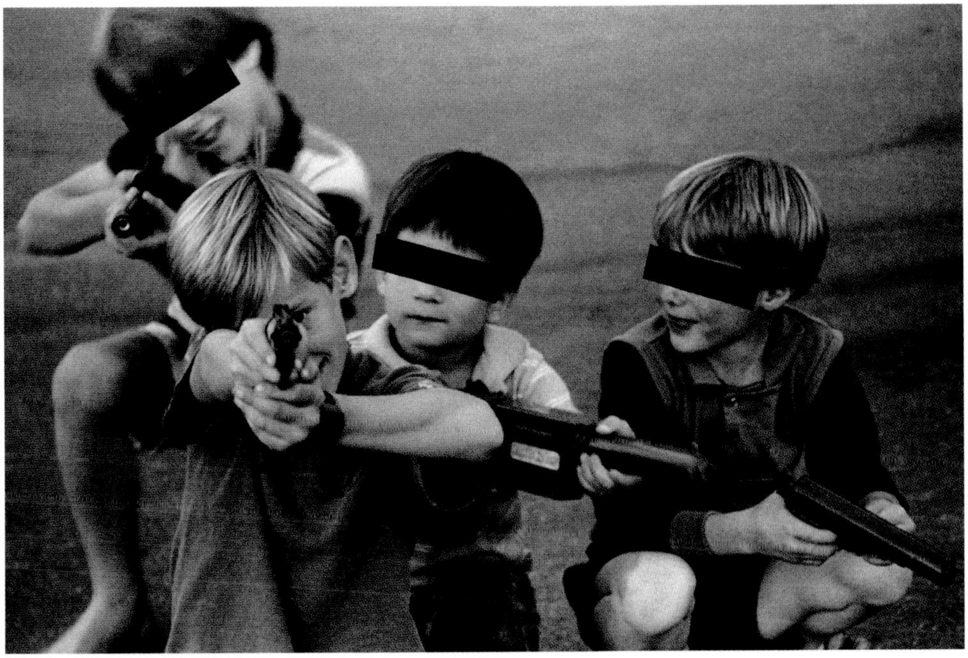

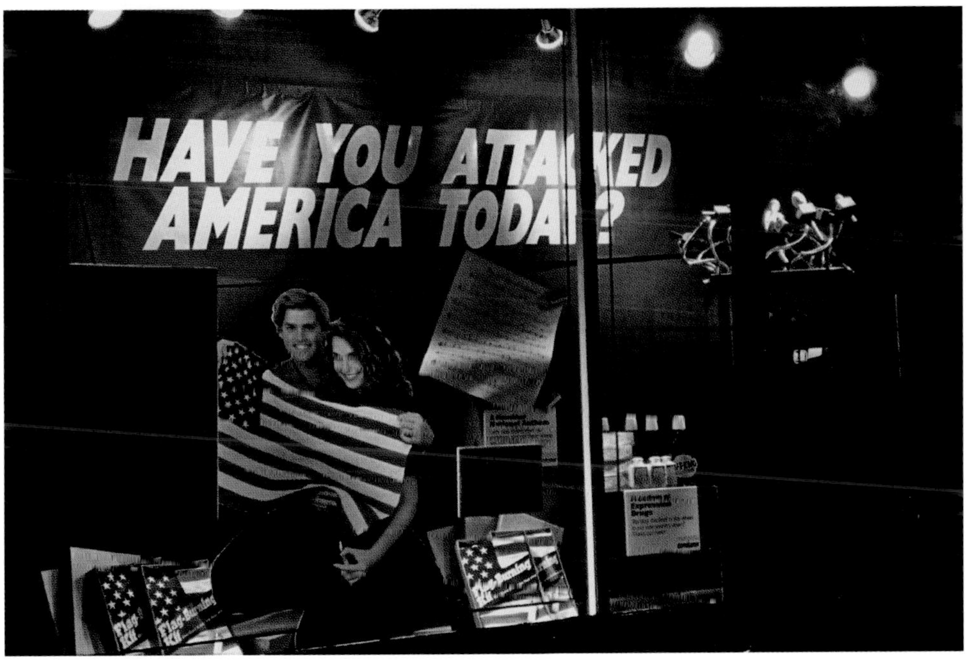
HAVE YOU
AMERICA

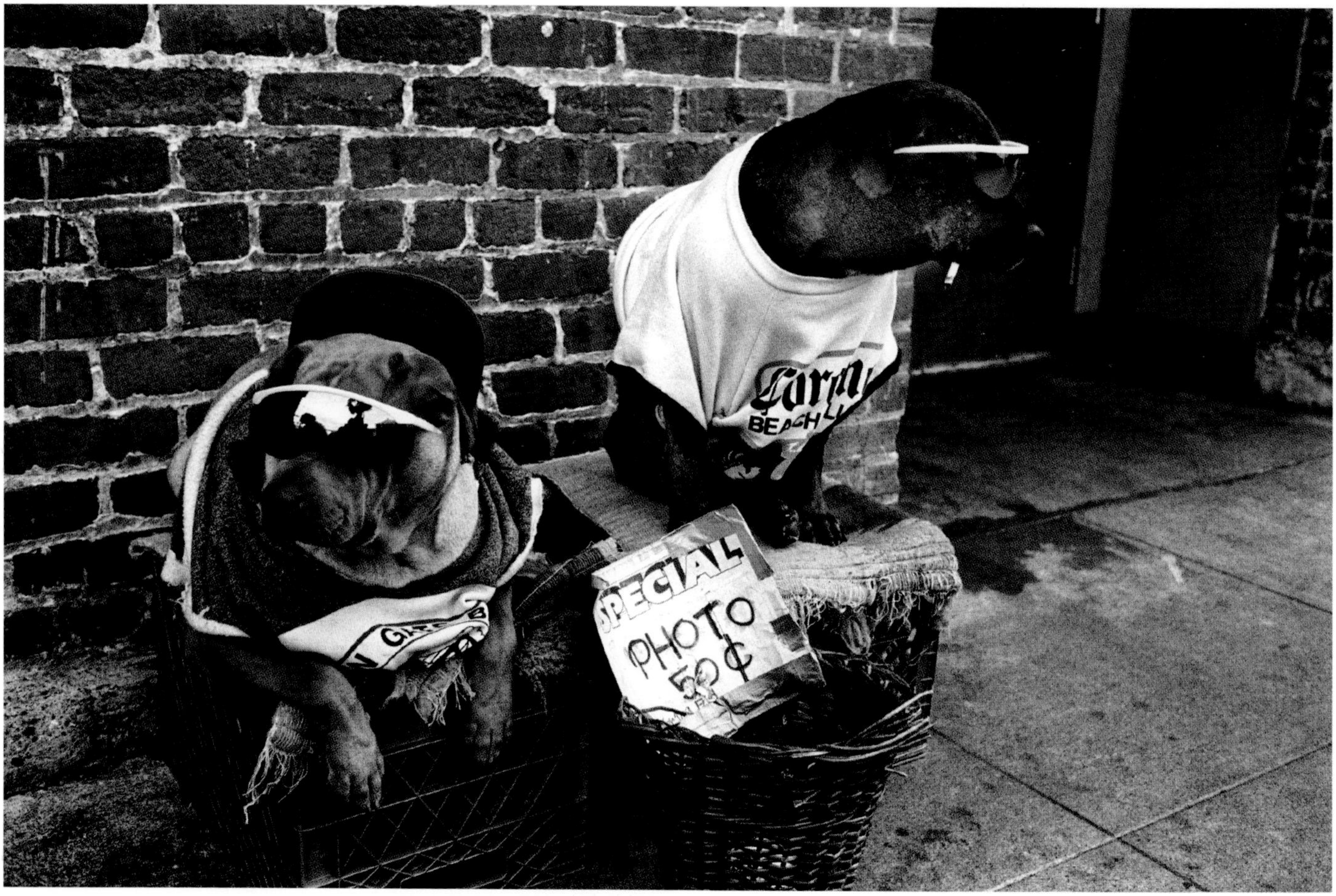
SPECIAL
PHOTO
BEACH

I felt as though I were present at an Ovidian metamorphosis:

the man's face was still too expressive, it retained that faintly annoying mimicry of intelligence by which you can recognize a French face anywhere.

But he would soon be a tree or a rock.

I wondered with some curiosity what powerful forces had to be brought into play to achieve such integrations and disintegrations so surely and swiftly.

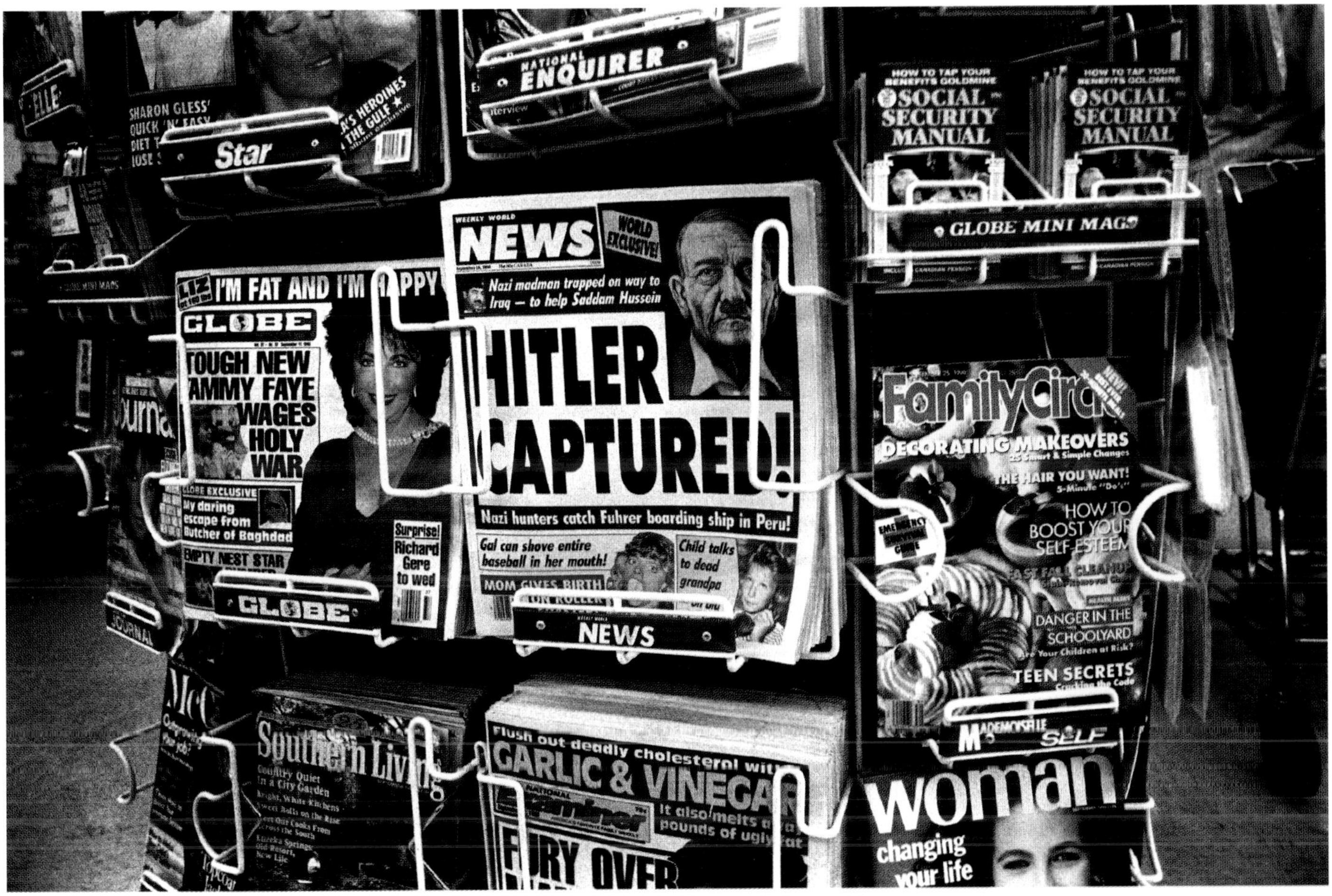
SHARON GLESS'
Star
NATIONAL ENQUIRER
HOW TO TAP YOUR BENEFITS GOLDMINE
SOCIAL SECURITY MANUAL
HOW TO TAP YOUR BENEFITS GOLDMINE
SOCIAL SECURITY MANUAL
GLOBE MINI MAG
I'M FAT AND I'M
GLOBE
TOUGH NEW
WAGES HOLY WAR
My daring escape from Butcher of Baghdad
Surprise! Richard Gere to wed
GLOBE
WEEKLY WORLD
NEWS
WORLD EXCLUSIVE!
Nazi madman trapped on way to Iraq — to help Saddam Hussein
HITLER CAPTURED!
Nazi hunters catch Fuhrer boarding ship in Peru!
Gal can shove entire baseball in her mouth!
Child talks to dead grandpa
MOM GIVES BIRTH
NEWS
FamilyCircle
DECORATING MAKEOVERS
25 Smart & Simple Changes
THE HAIR YOU WANT!
5-Minute "Do's"
HOW TO BOOST YOUR SELF-ESTEEM
DANGER IN THE SCHOOLYARD
Are Your Children at Risk?
TEEN SECRETS
SELF
Southern Living
Flush out deadly cholesterol with
GARLIC & VINEGAR
It also melts
pounds of ugly
woman
changing your life

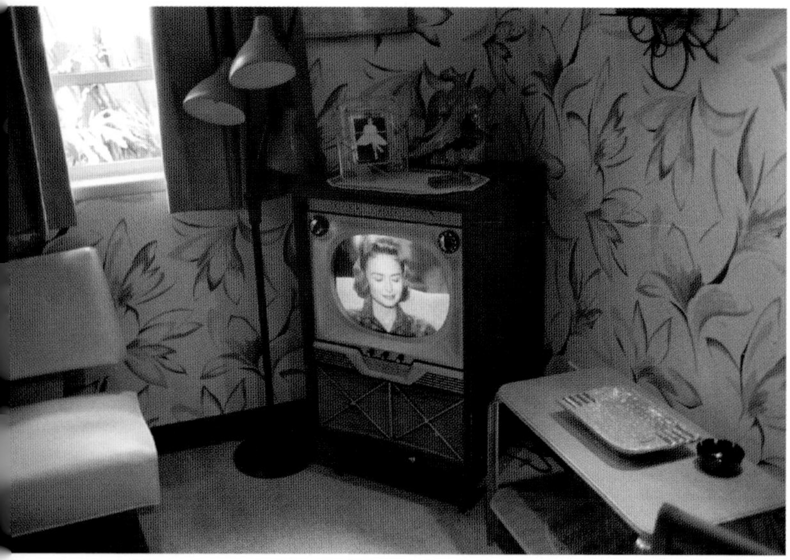

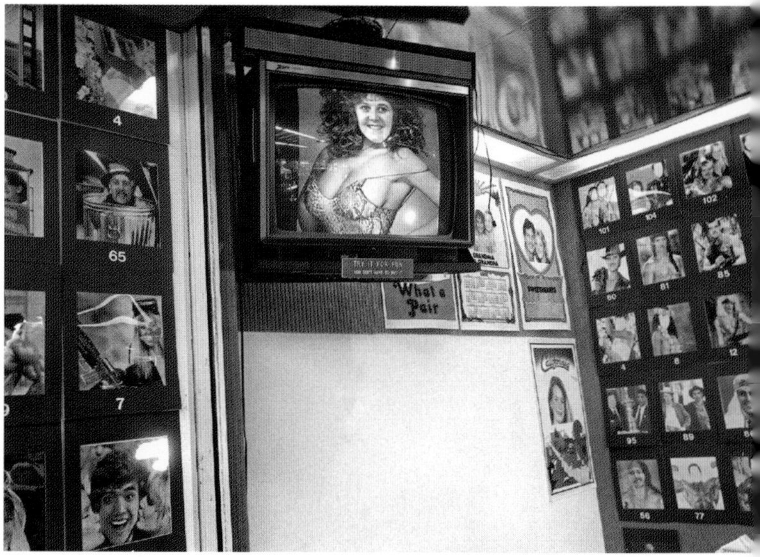
4
65
7
What a Pair

Now, these forces are mild and persuasive. You have only to walk the streets, enter a shop or switch on a radio to encounter them, to feel their effect on you like a warm breath.

In America—at least the America I know—you are never alone in the street.

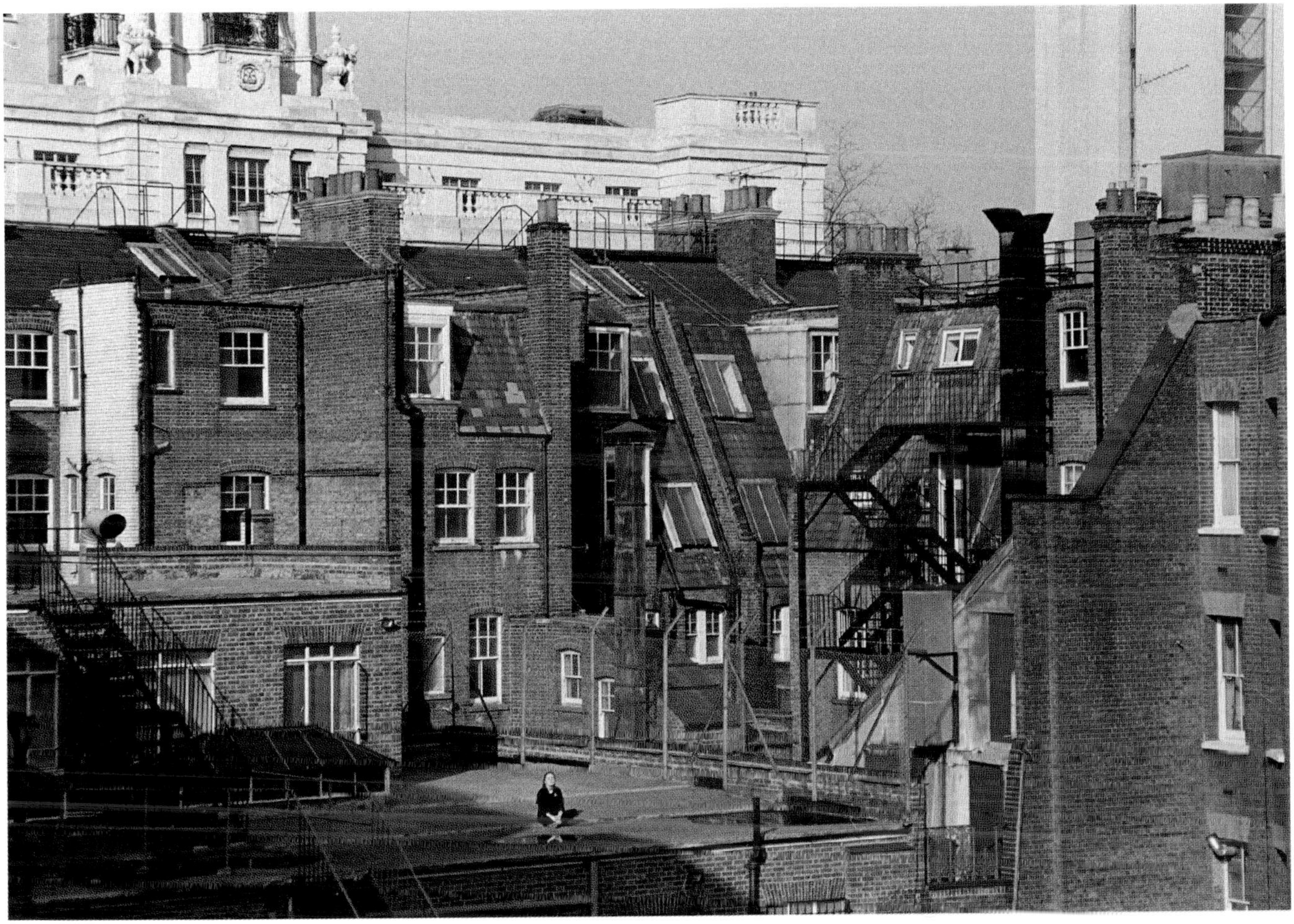

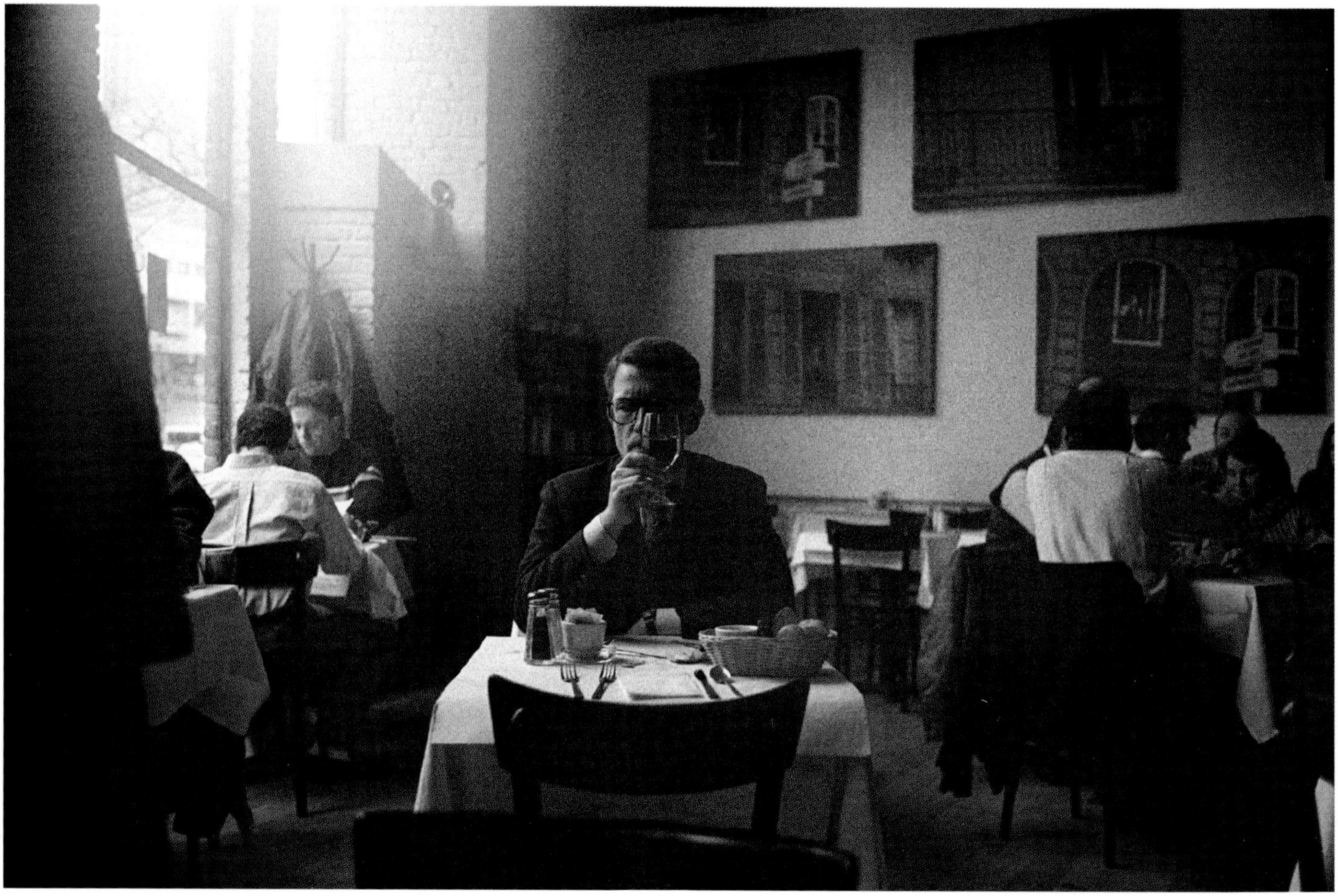

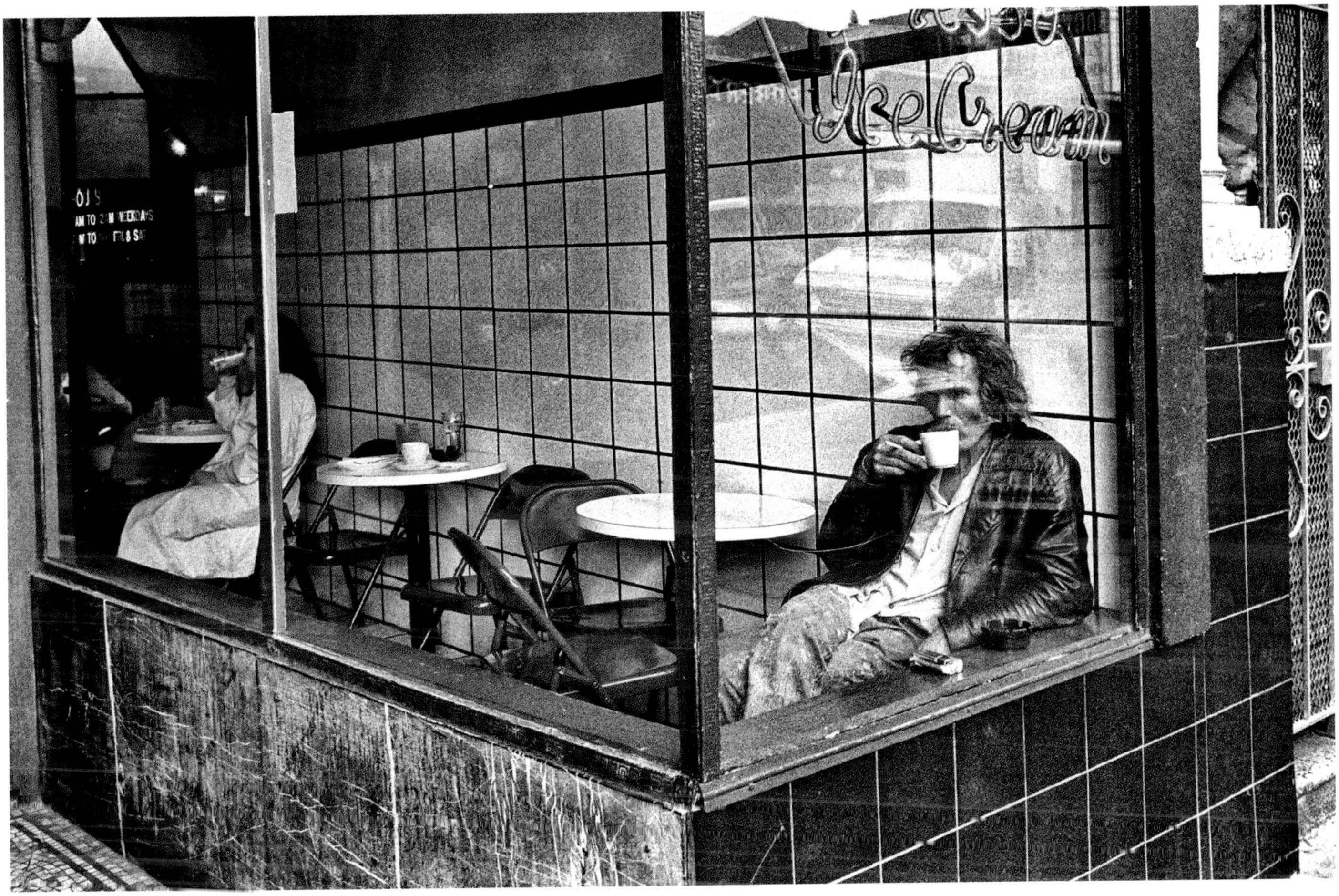
Ice Cream

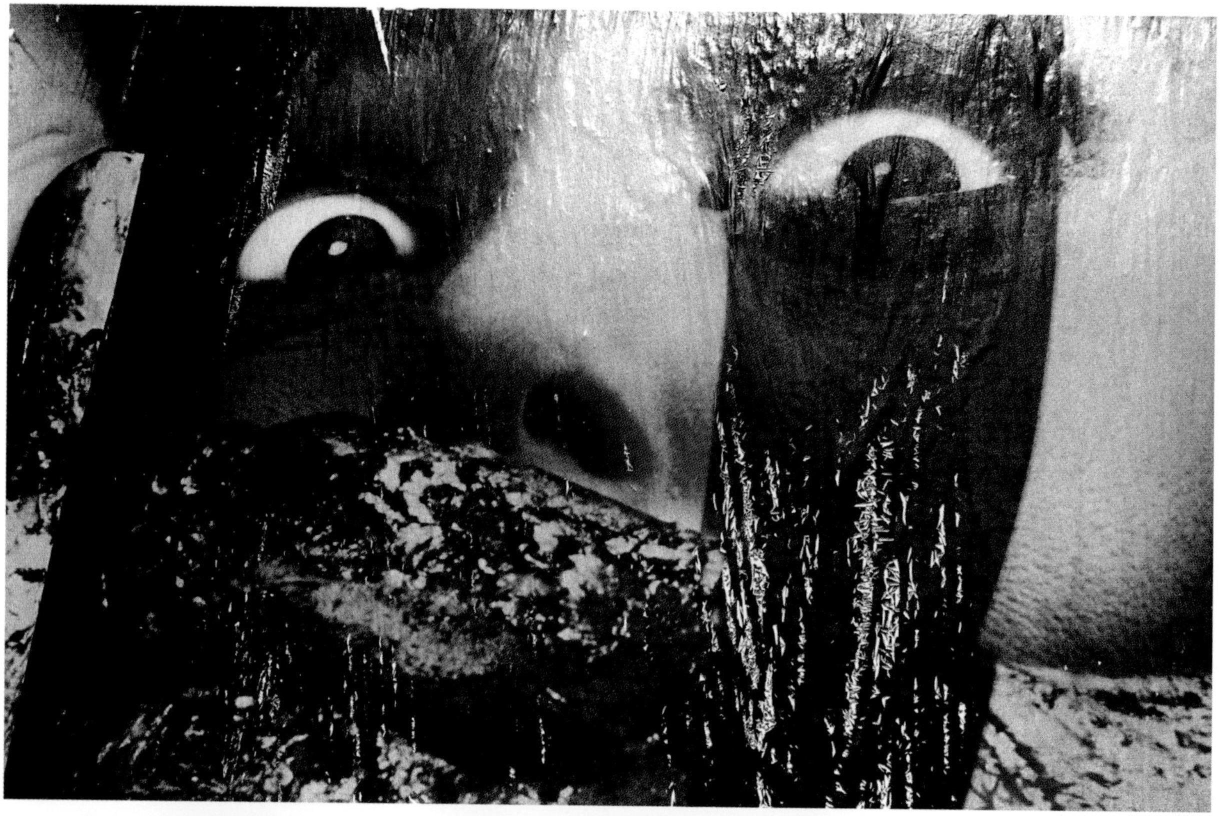

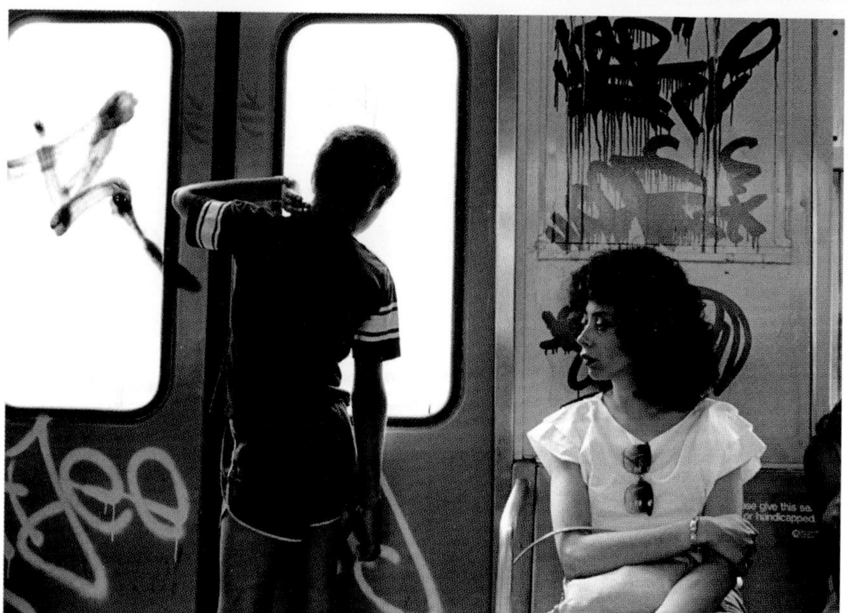

The walls speak to you.

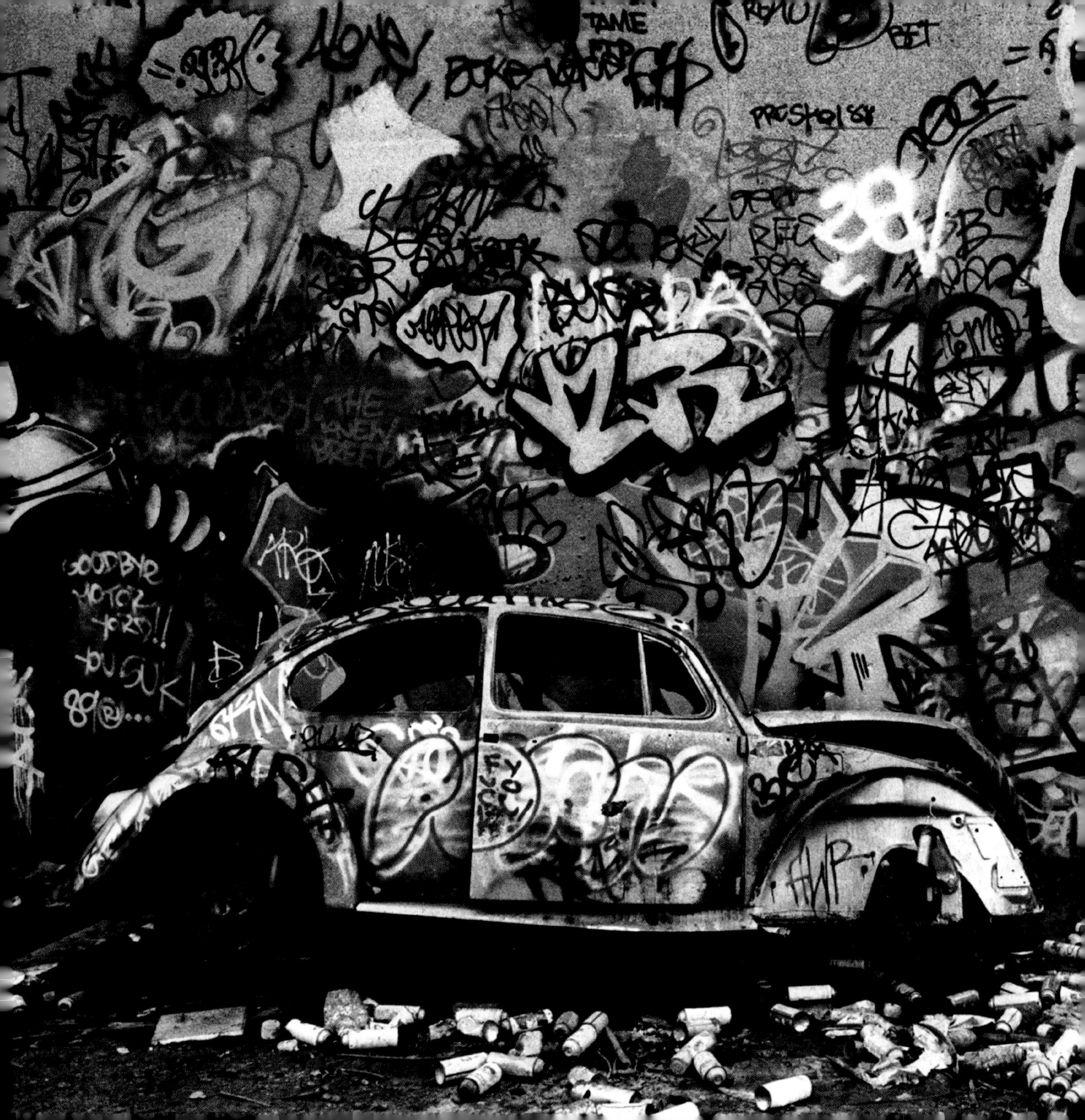

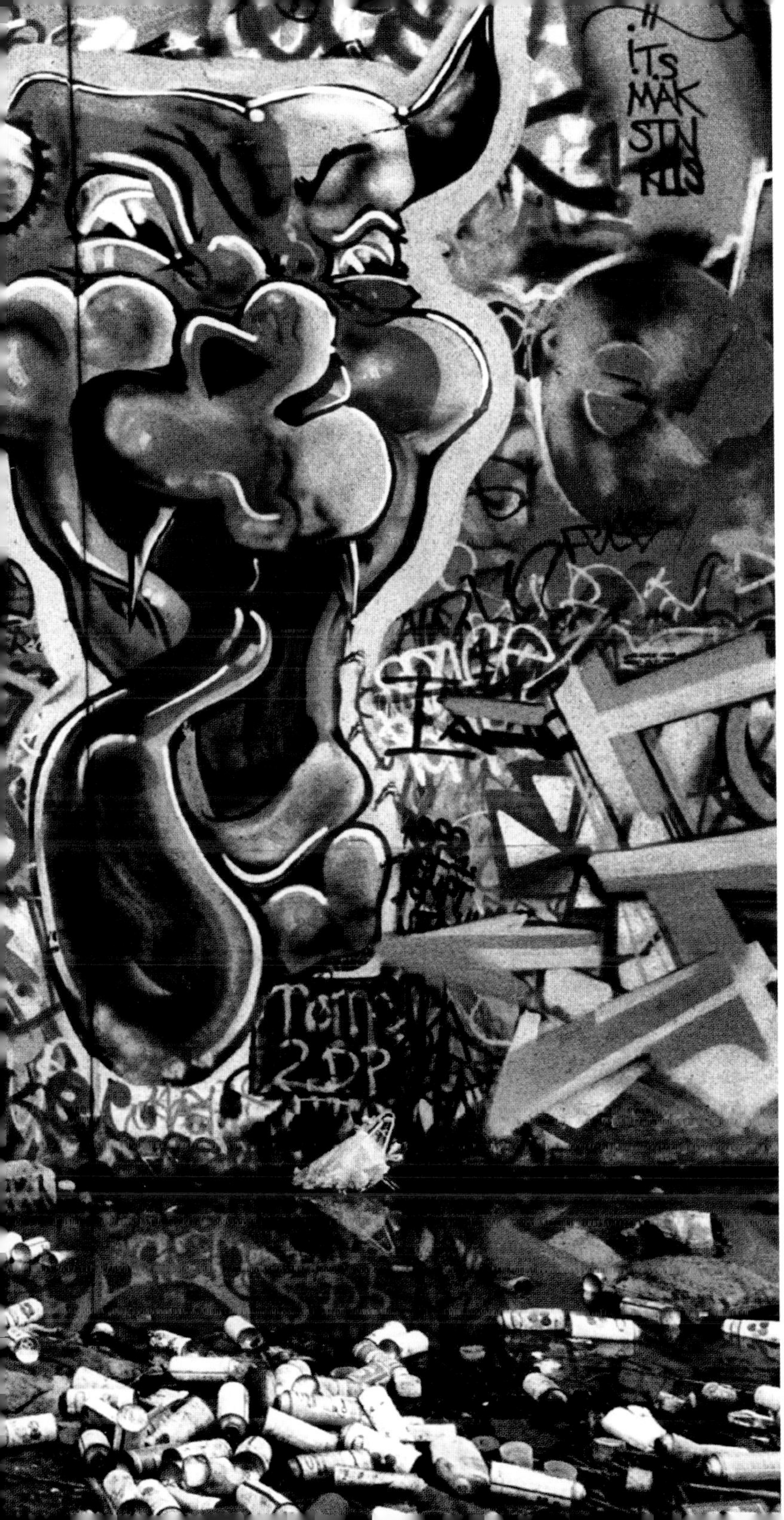

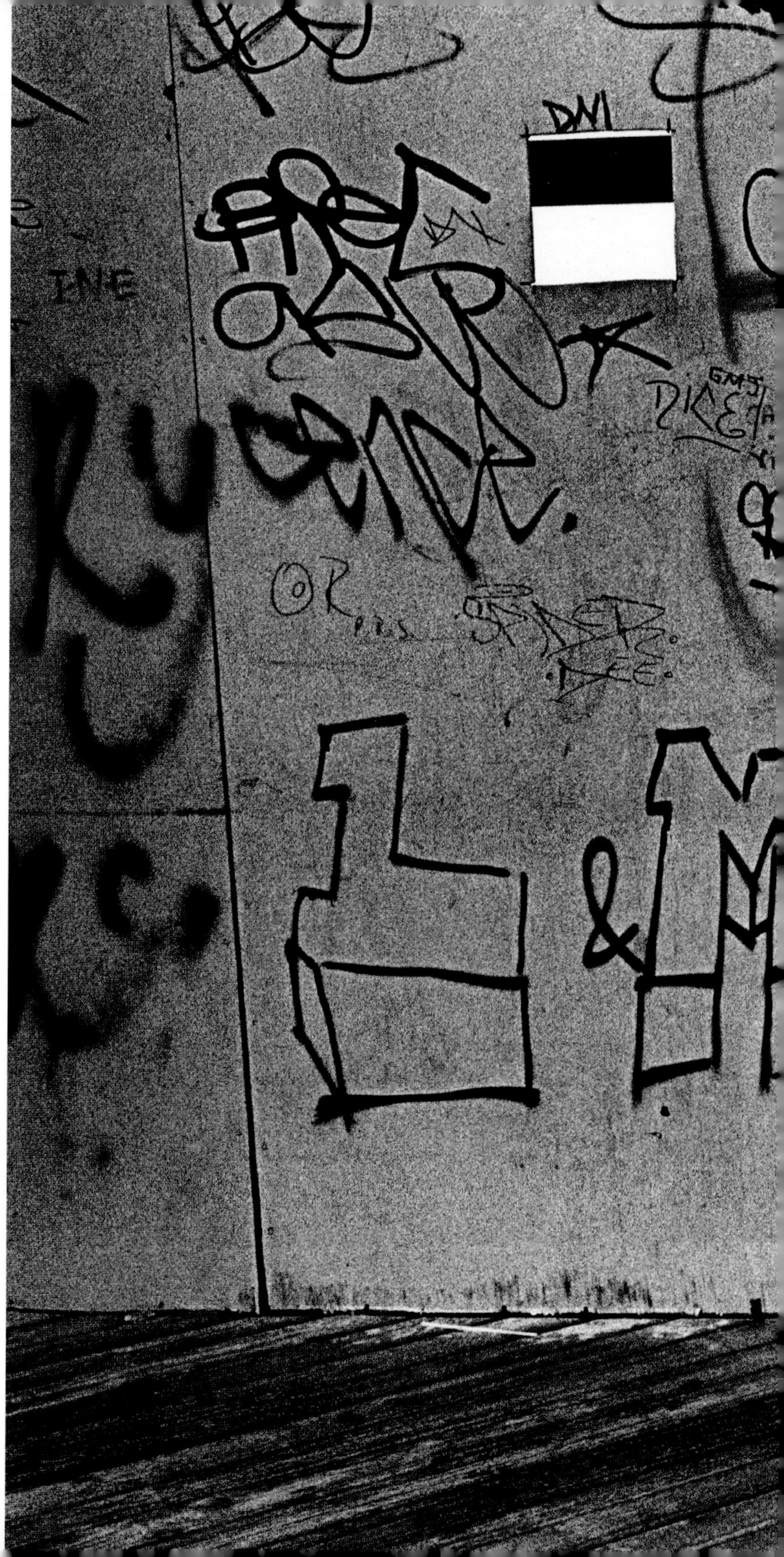
DNI

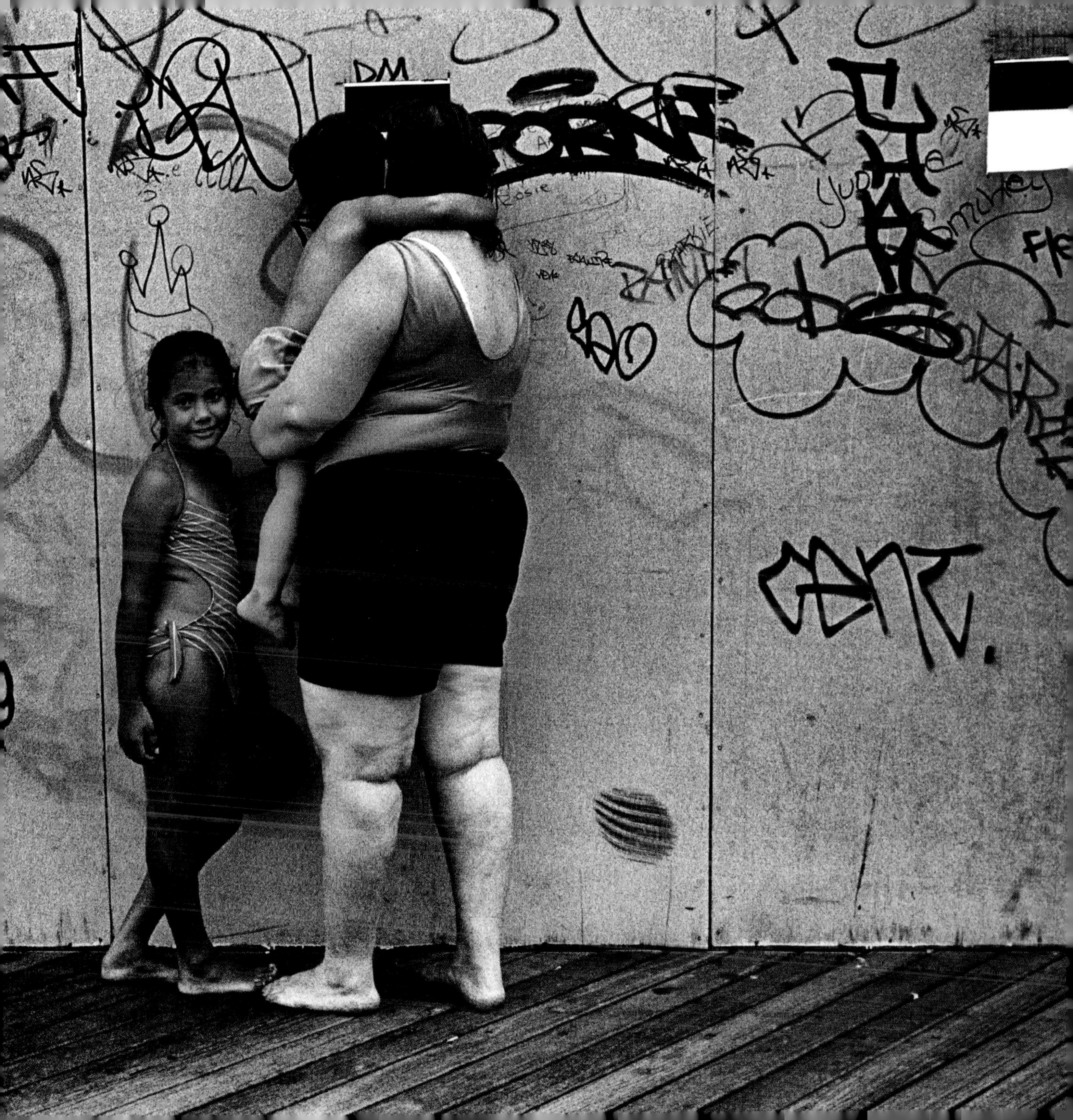

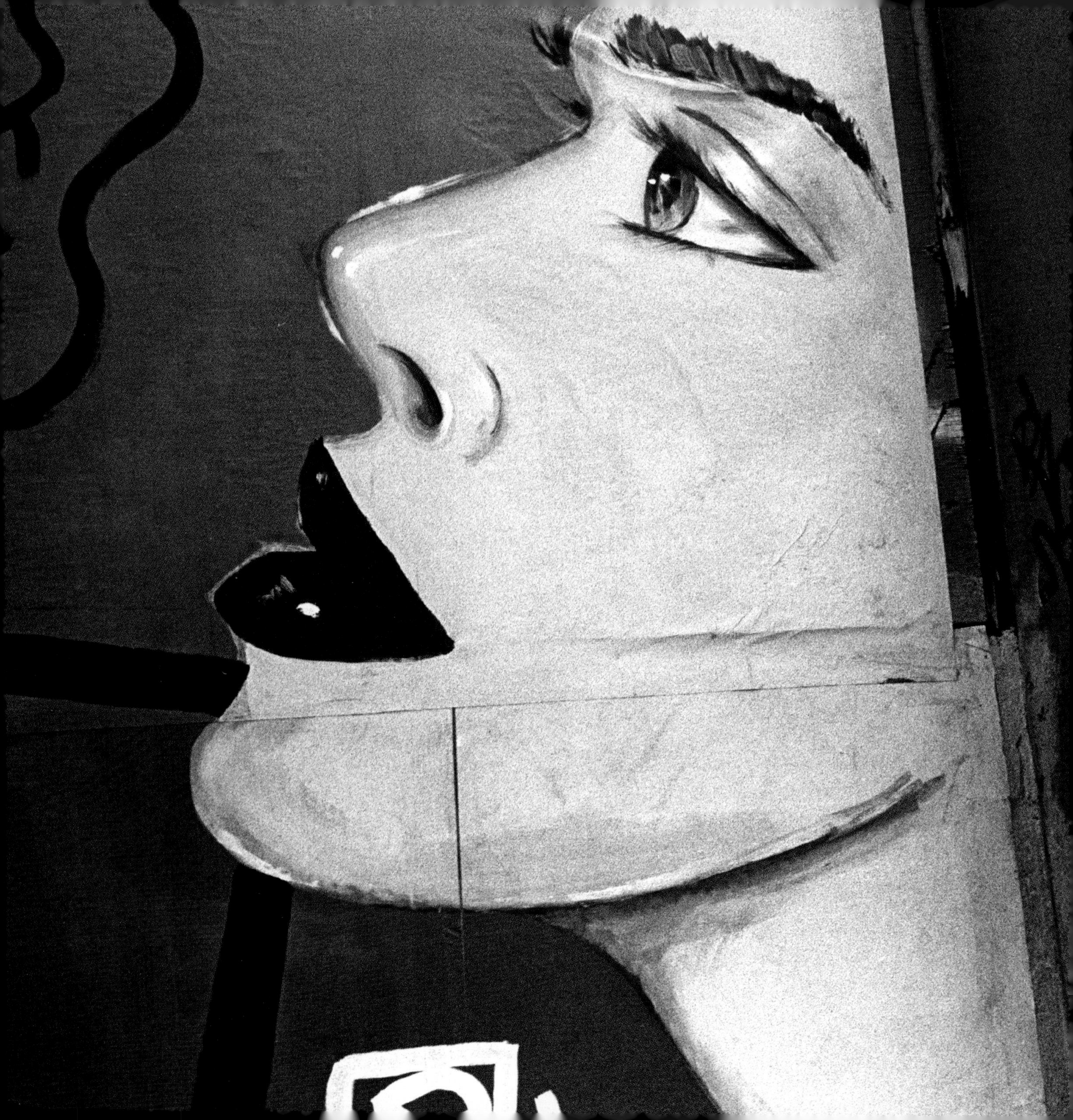

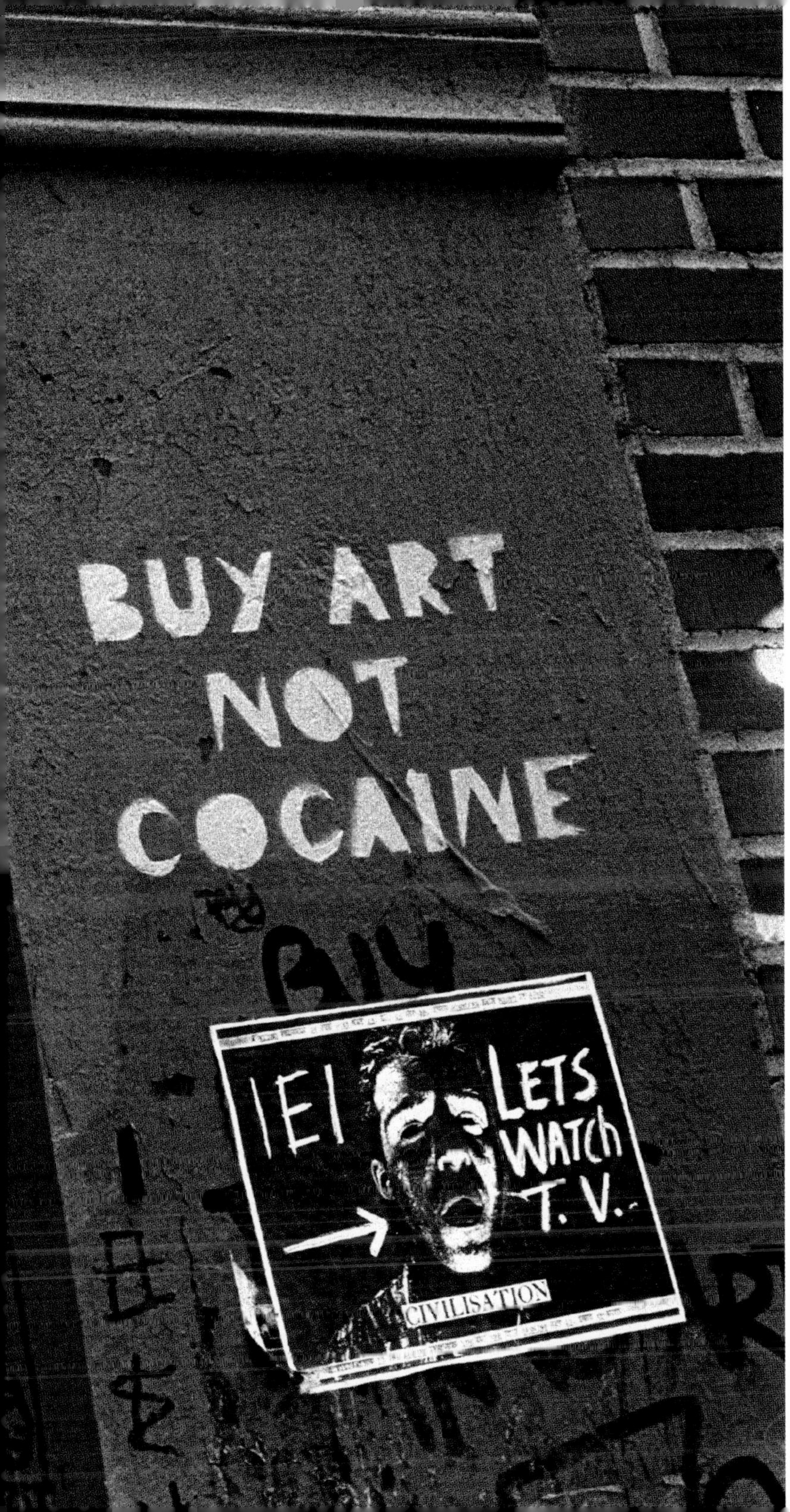
BUY ART
NOT
COCAINE
BUY
IEI
LETS
WATCH
T.V.
CIVILISATION

To left and right of you there are posters, illuminated advertisements and enormous shop windows simply containing large boards with photomontages or tables of statistics. Here, you have a distraught woman leaning over to kiss an American soldier, there, a plane dropping bombs on a village, and, beneath the picture, the words, 'Bibles, not bombs'

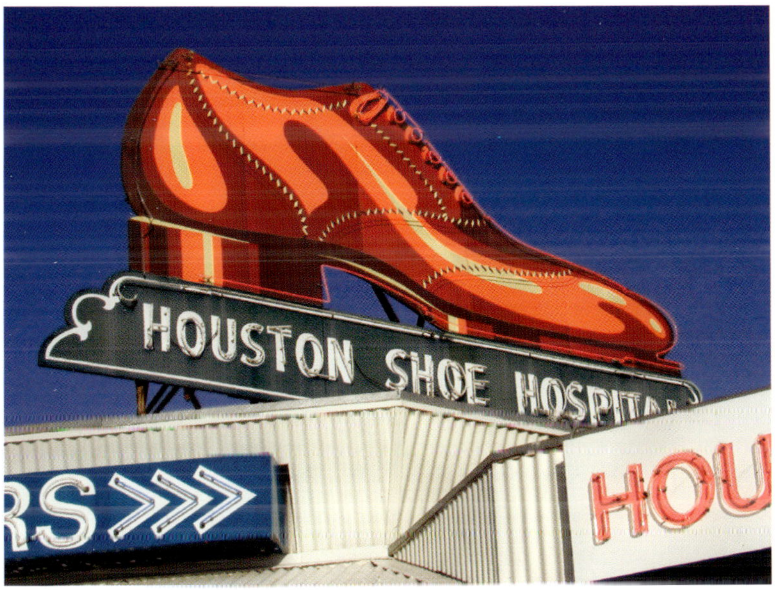
HOUSTON SHOE HOSPITAL
RS
HOU

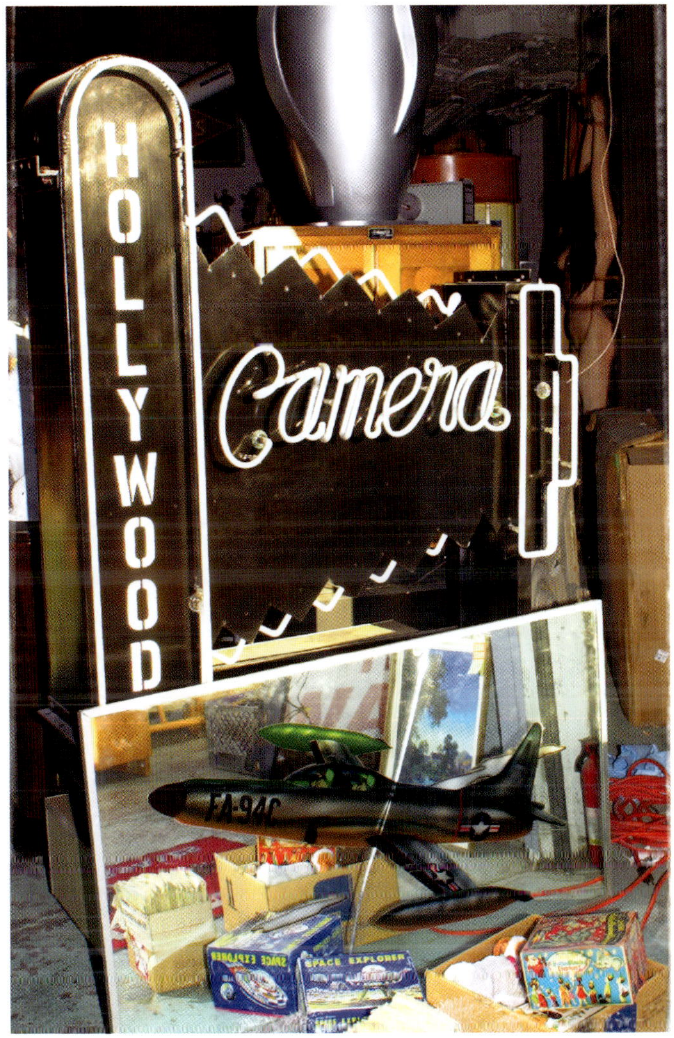
HOLLYWOOD
Camera
FA-94C
SPACE EXPLORER
SPACE EXPLORER

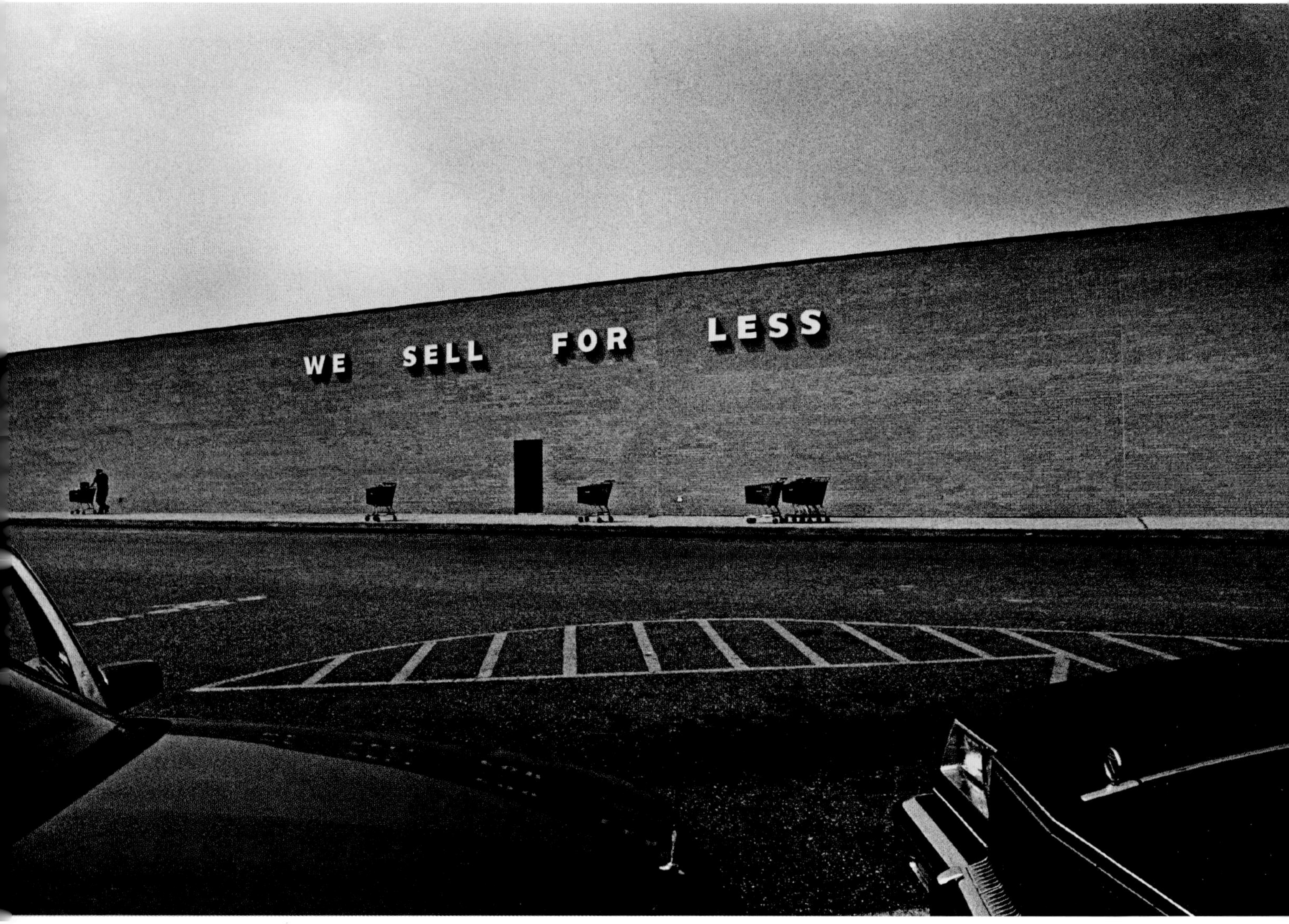
WE SELL FOR LESS

The nation walks with you.

It proffers advice and commands. But it does so sotto voce and is careful to explain its orders in minute detail. There is no injunction that is not accompanied by a brief commentary or a justificatory image, whether in an advert for cosmetics (Today, more than ever, you have to be beautiful. Take care of your face for when he comes home: buy cream X.) or in propaganda for War Bonds.

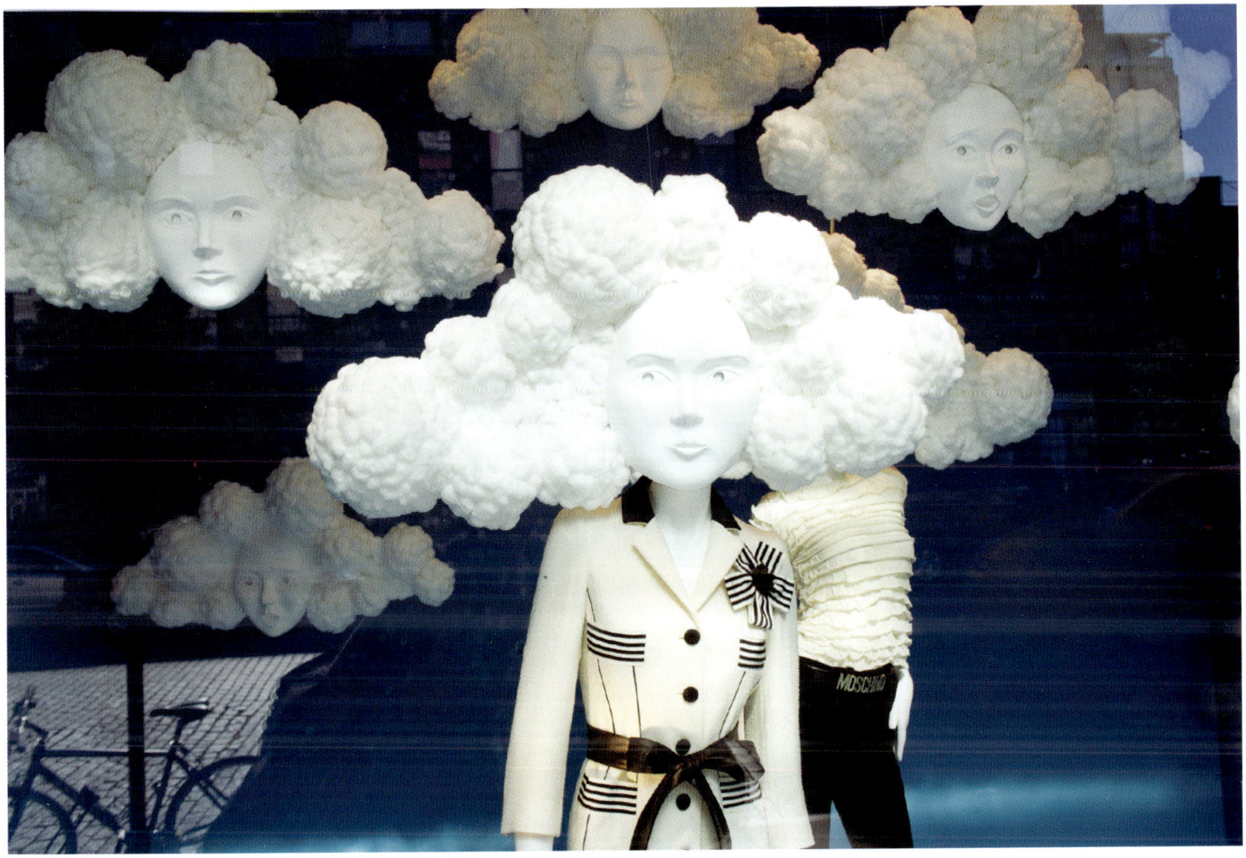
MOSCHINO

I dined yesterday in a restaurant at Fontana, an artificial village built around a great dam in Tennessee.

All along the road leading to that dam, a road full of lorries, automobiles and pick-up trucks, a great hoarding conveys a parable in cartoon form on the subject of working together. Two donkeys roped together are trying to reach two piles of hay some distance apart. Each pulls on the rope in its own direction and they are half-strangling each other. Finally, they understand. They move together and begin merrily munching the first pile together. When they have eaten it, we see them starting out in unison towards the second.

Clearly, it was a deliberate decision to banish all commentary. The passers-by have to draw the conclusion themselves. No violence is done to them. On the contrary, the image is an appeal to their intelligence. They are obliged to interpret and understand it. It does not bludgeon them, as Nazi propaganda did with its garish posters. It remains low-key. It requires participation if it is to be deciphered. When they have understood, it is as though they had formed the idea themselves. They are already more than half convinced.

In the factories, they have put up loudspeakers everywhere. These are intended to combat the workers' isolation in their encounter with matter.

Walking through the immense naval dockyard near Baltimore, you first encounter that human dispersal, that great solitude of the workers so familiar to us in Europe. Masked men, bending over steel plates, spend all day working with their oxyhydrogen torches. But as soon as they put on their headphones, they can hear music.

And the music is already guidance insinuating itself stealthily into them, it is already a guided dream.

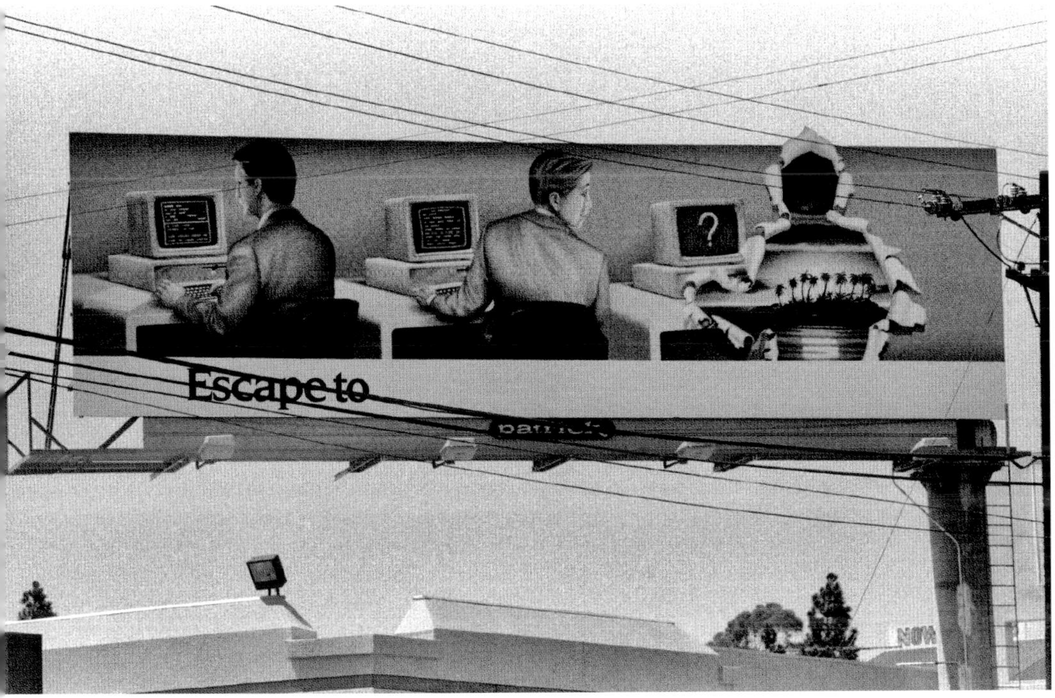
Escape to

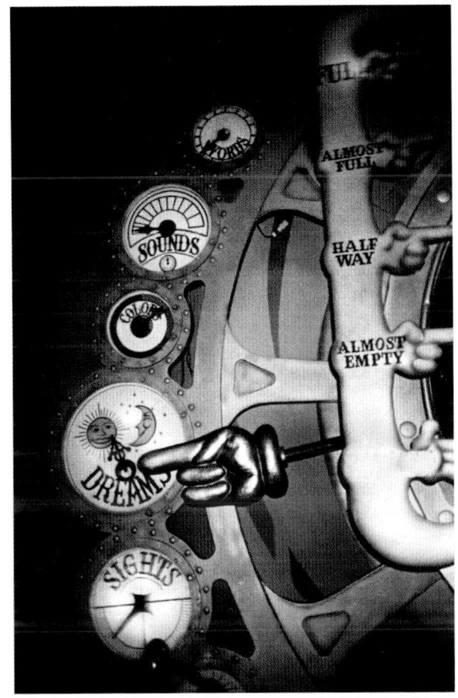
ALMOST FULL
HALF WAY
ALMOST EMPTY
SOUNDS
DREAMS
SIGHTS

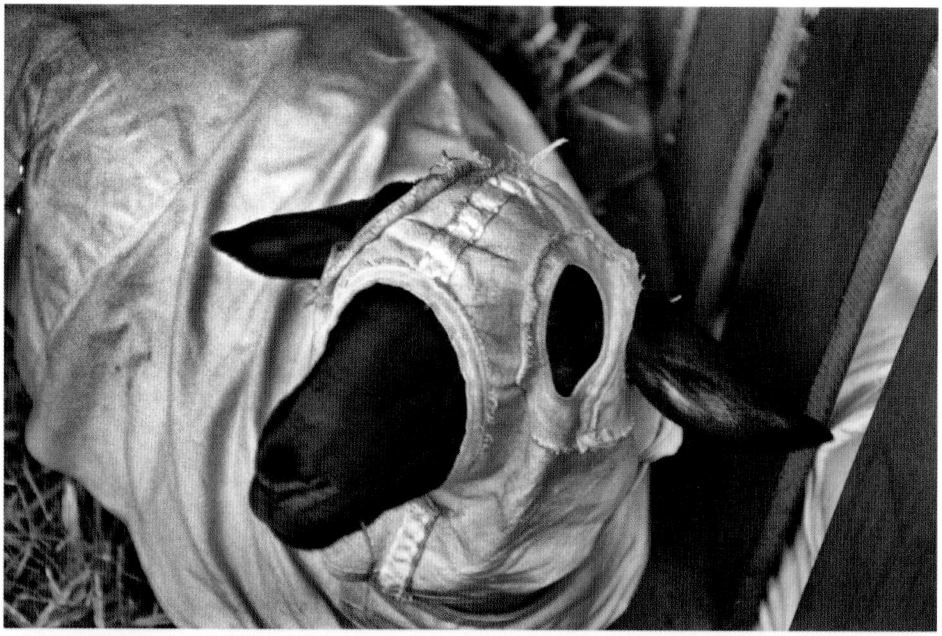

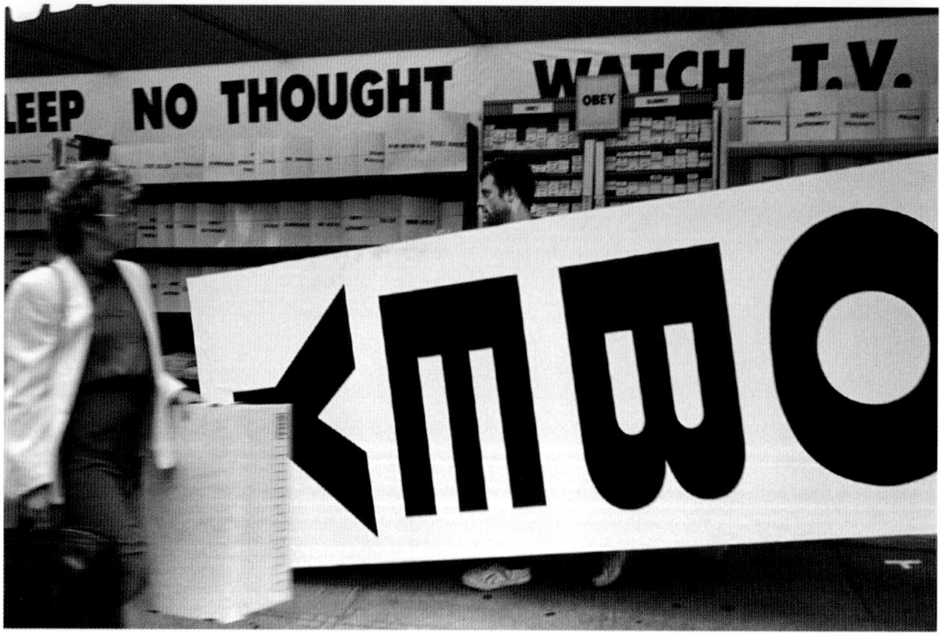
LEEP
NO THOUGHT
WATCH T.V.
OBEY

And then the music stops and they receive information about the war or their work.

When we left Fontana, the engineer who had so kindly taken us everywhere led us into a little glass room where a new wax disc was revolving, readied for the recording of our voices. He explained that all the visitors who had visited the dam had summed up their impressions at the microphone before they left. We were not about to refuse such a kind host. Those of us who knew English spoke and our words were recorded. The next day they would be broadcast in the dockyard, in the canteen and to all the houses in the village, and the workers would be encouraged to continue their good work, learning with pleasure of the excellent impression they had made on a group of foreigners.

Add to this the advice meted out by the radio and in the columns of the newspapers and, particularly, the activities of the countless voluntary organizations whose aims are almost always educational, and you will see that the American citizen is tightly hedged about.

But it would be an error to see this as an oppressive manoeuvre on the part of the government or big American capitalists.

The present government is, of course, at war. It is obliged, for purposes of war propaganda, to use such methods. Doubtless, too, one of its main concerns is education.

In Tennessee, for example, where the farmers ruined the soil by the repeated planting of maize, it is trying to teach them gradually to allow the soil to rest by varying their crops each year. To achieve its goal, it has combined gifts (low-cost electricity, free irrigation) with argument. But what we have here is a much more spontaneous and diffuse phenomenon.

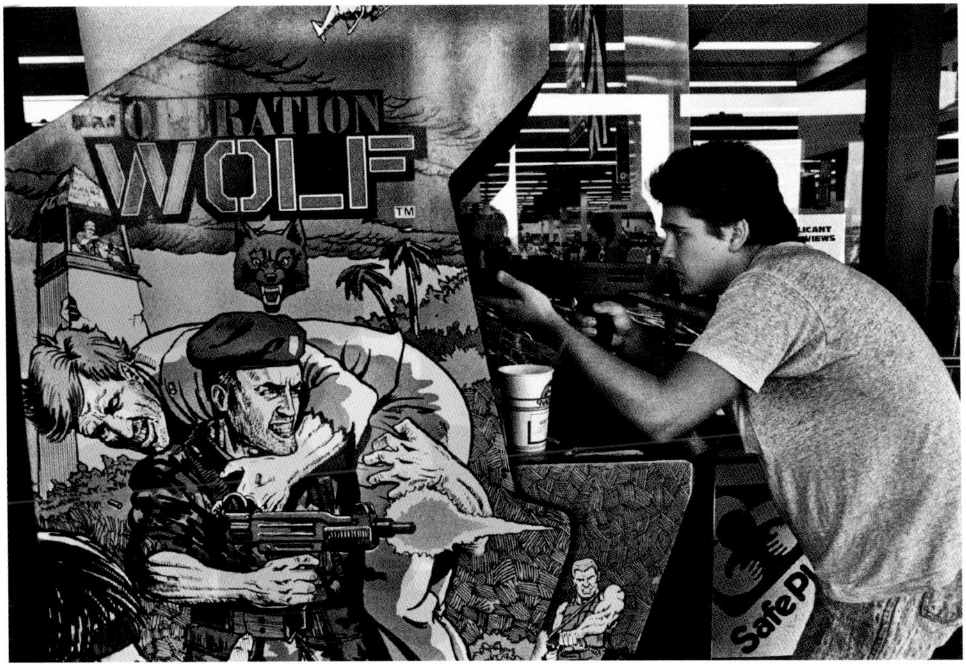
OPERATION
WOLF
TM
Safe Pl

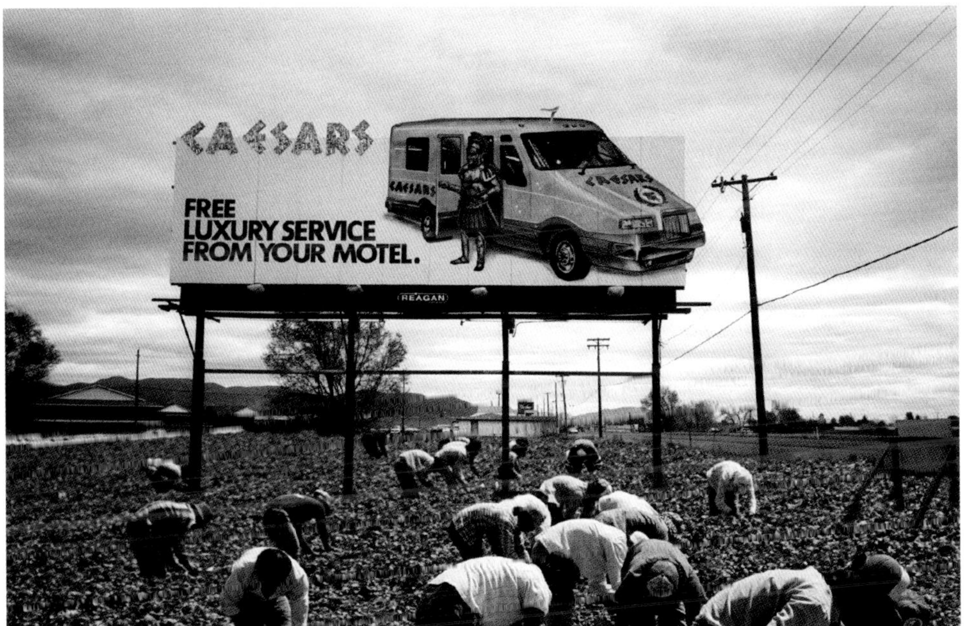
CAESARS
FREE
LUXURY SERVICE
FROM YOUR MOTEL.
REAGAN

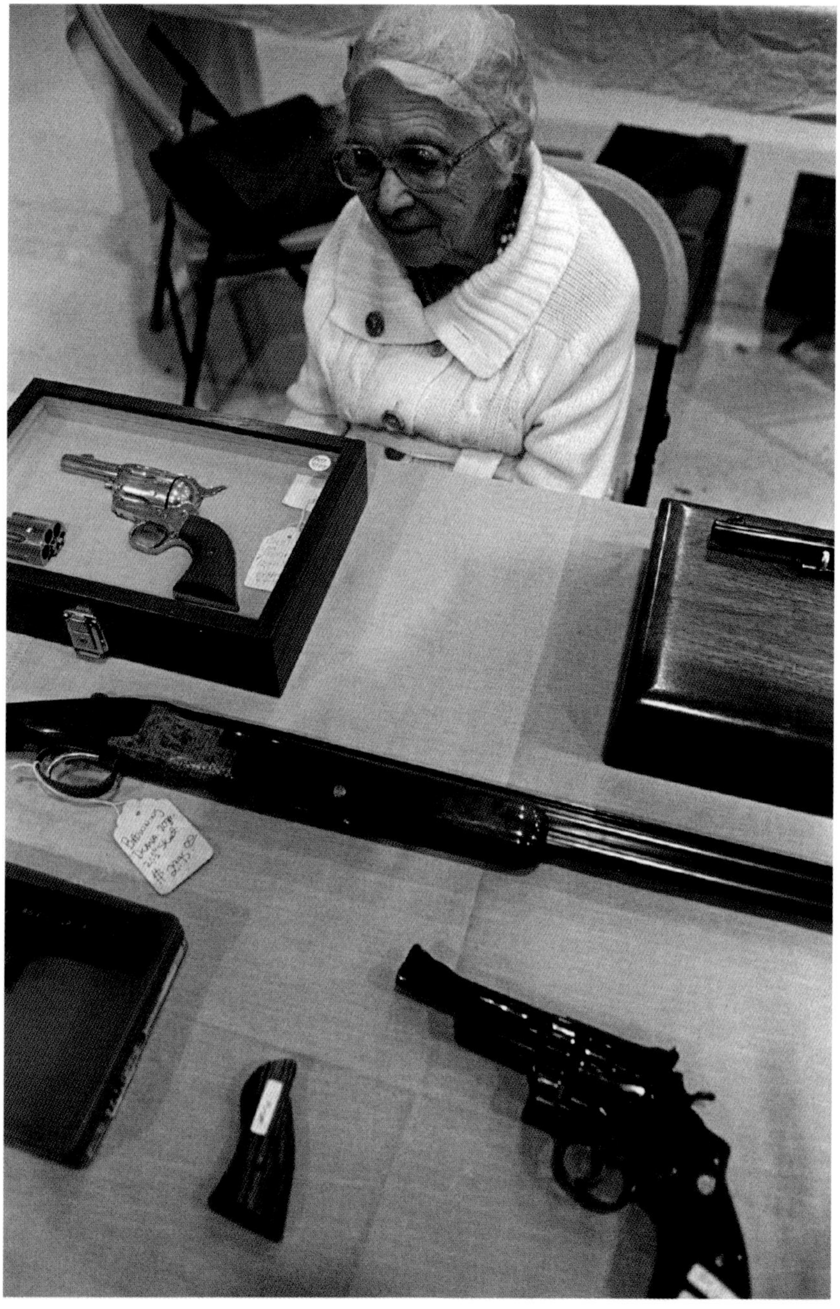

This educative tendency really springs from the heart of the community. Every American is educated by other Americans and educates others in turn.

All over New York, both in the schools and outside, there are courses in Americanization.

And they teach everything: sewing, cooking,

even romance.

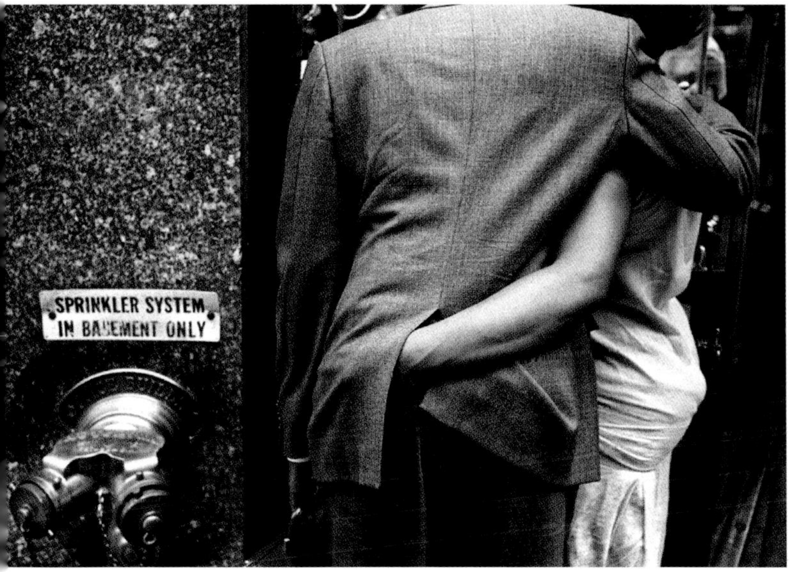
SPRINKLER SYSTEM
IN BASEMENT ONLY

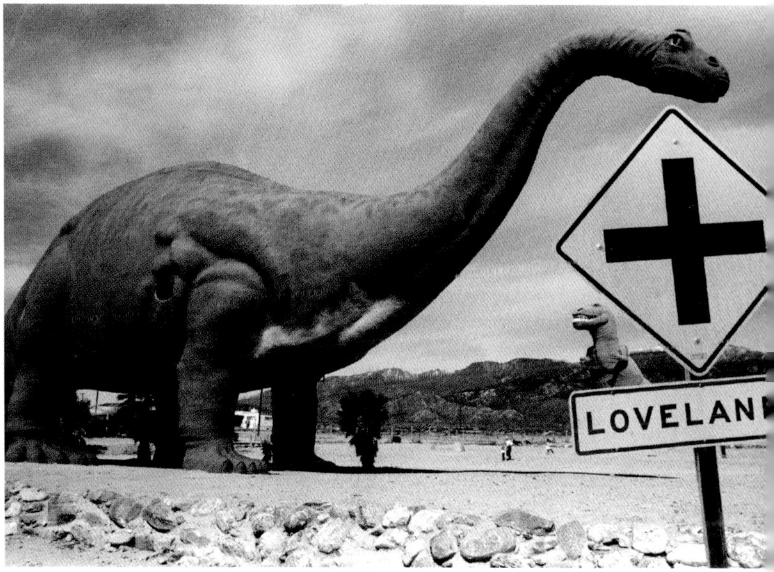
LOVELAN

There is a course in a New York school on how a girl should go about getting her boyfriend to marry her.

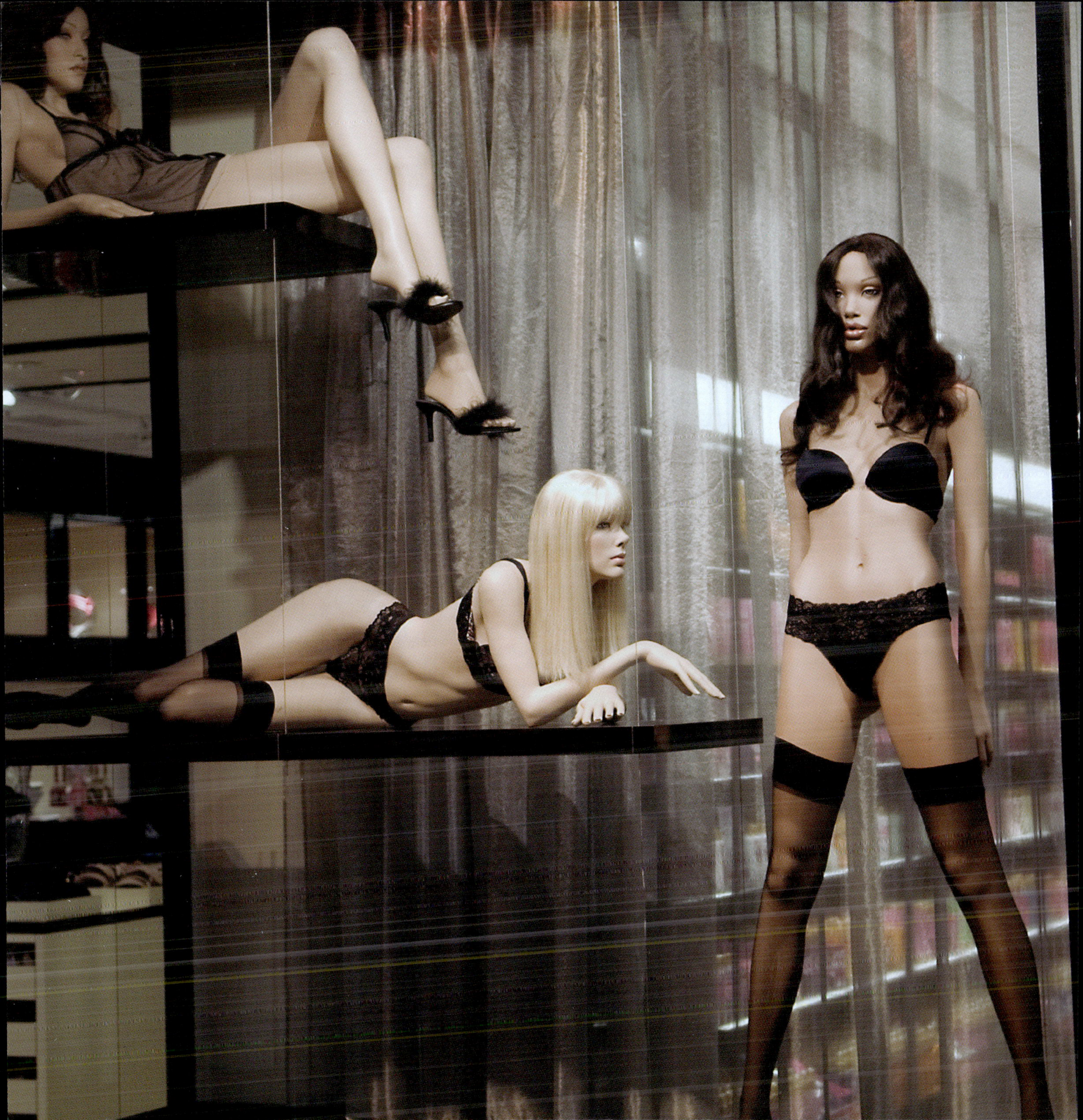

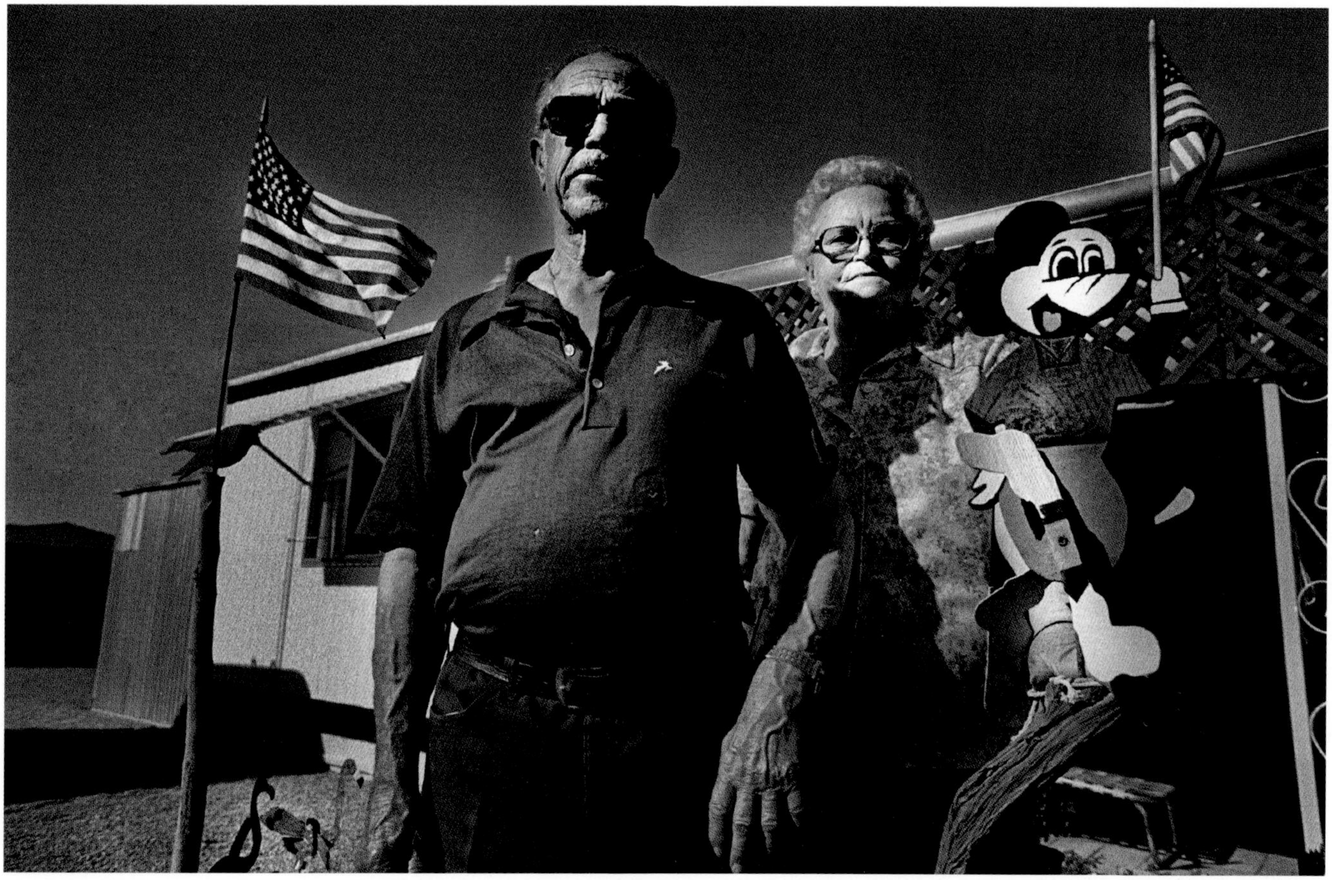

In all this, it is not so much a question of training a human being as training a pure American. But Americans make no distinction between American reason and reason tout court. All the advice with which their route is studded is so perfectly motivated, so penetrating, that they feel themselves cradled by an immense solicitude that never leaves them helpless or alone.

I have met some of these 'modern' mothers who have never ordered their children to do anything without first persuading them to obey. They have acquired a more total, and perhaps more formidable, authority over them than if they had used threats and blows. In the same way, the American, whose reason and freedom are appealed to at every hour of the day, makes it a point of honour to do what he is asked. It is by acting like everyone else that he feels both most reasonable and most American; it is by displaying the greatest conformism that he feels most free.

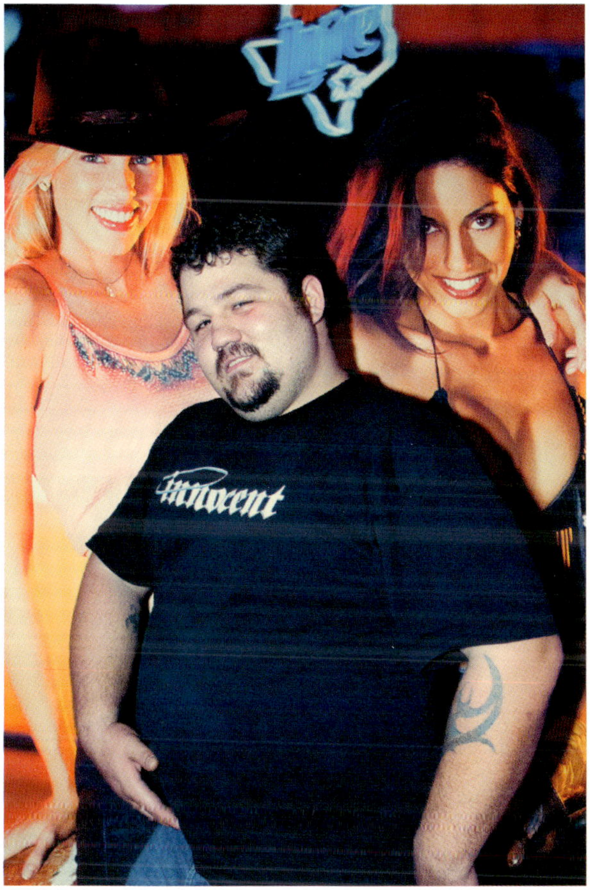
innocent

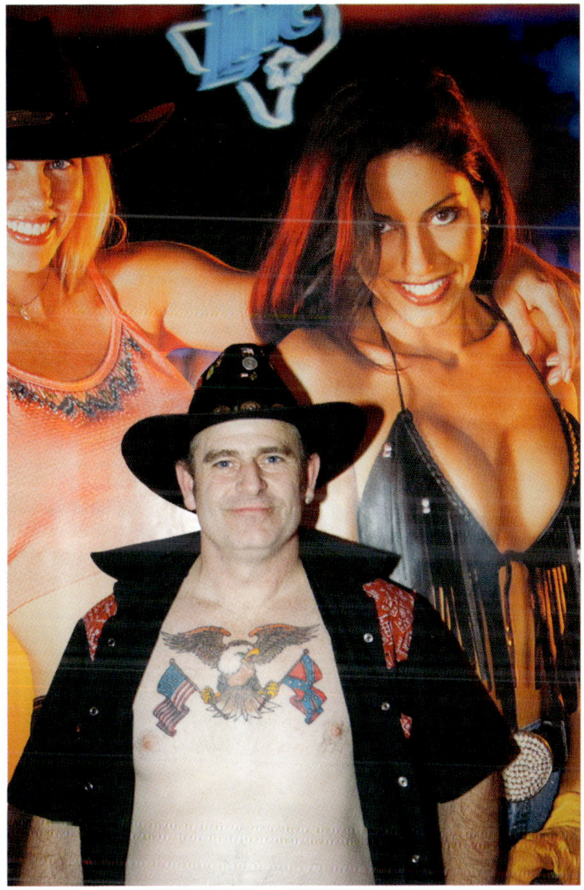

So far as I can judge, the characteristics of the American nation are the opposite of those which Hitler gave to Germany and Maurras wanted to give to France.

For Hitler (or Maurras), an argument is good for Germany if, first of all, it is German. It is always suspect if it has any slight whiff of universality.

By contrast, it is the peculiar characteristic of the American that he regards his thought as universal. One can detect a Puritan influence here which I need not go into at this point. But there is, above all, this concrete, daily presence of a flesh-and-blood Reason, a Reason you can see. Most of the people I spoke to seemed to have a naive, passionate faith in the virtues of Reason.

One evening an American said to me, 'If international politics were carried on by reasonable, sane men, wouldn't war be abolished forever?' Some French people present pointed out that the matter was not so straightforward and he grew angry. 'All right,' he said, with indignant contempt, 'go and build graveyards!' I, for my part, said nothing. Discussion between us was not possible.

I believe in evil and he does not.

It is this Rousseauesque optimism which distances the American from our standpoint where Nazi Germany is concerned. In order to accept the atrocities, he would have to accept that man can be wholly evil. 'Do you believe there are two Germanies?' an American doctor asked me. I replied that I did not.

'I understand,' he said. 'You can't think otherwise because France has suffered so much. But it's a pity.'

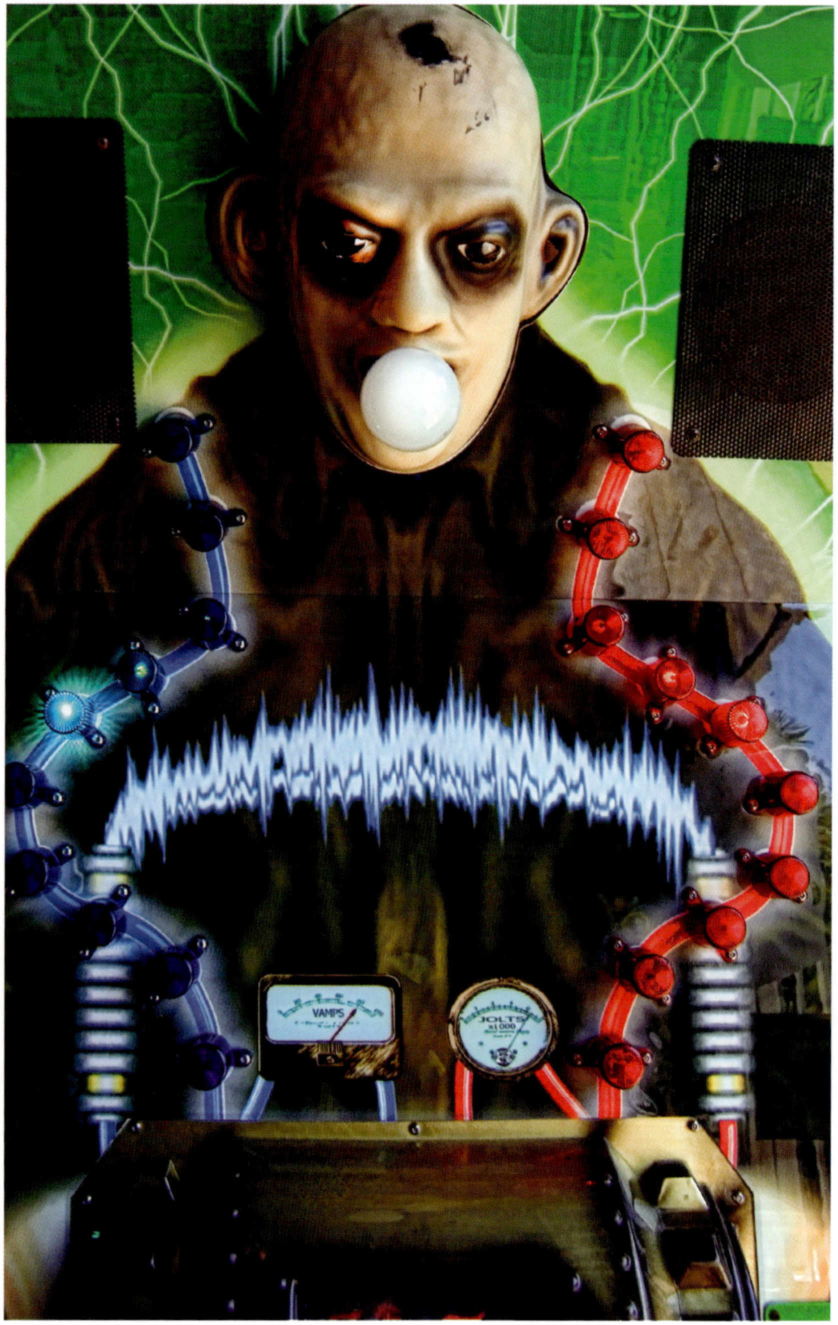
VAMPS
JOLTS
x1000

Machines play a part here. They too are universalizing factors.

With mechanical objects, there is generally only one way to use them; the one indicated in the accompanying leaflet. The American uses his mechanical corkscrew, his fridge or his automobile at the same time as all the other Americans and in the same way. Besides, the object is not made to order. It is for anyone and will work for anyone, provided he knows how to use it properly.

So, when the American puts his nickel in the slot in the tram, the subway or the drinks machine, he feels like anyone.

Not like an anonymous unit, but like a person who has divested himself of his individuality and elevated himself to the impersonality of the Universal.

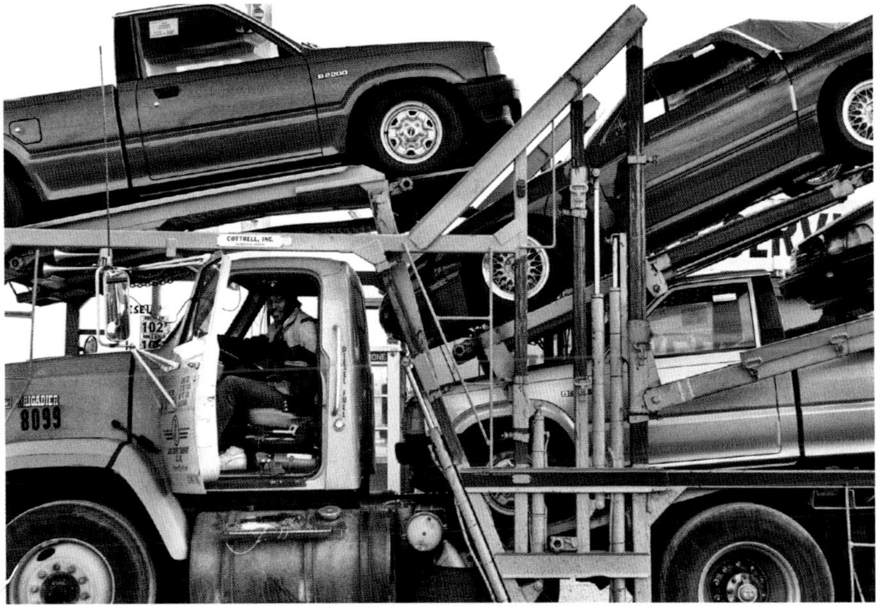
B2200
COTTRELL, INC.
8099

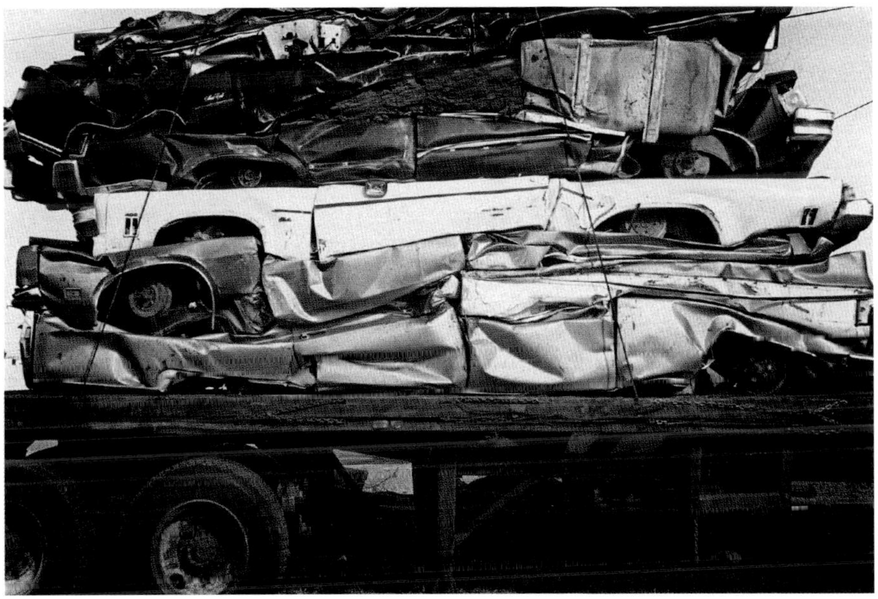

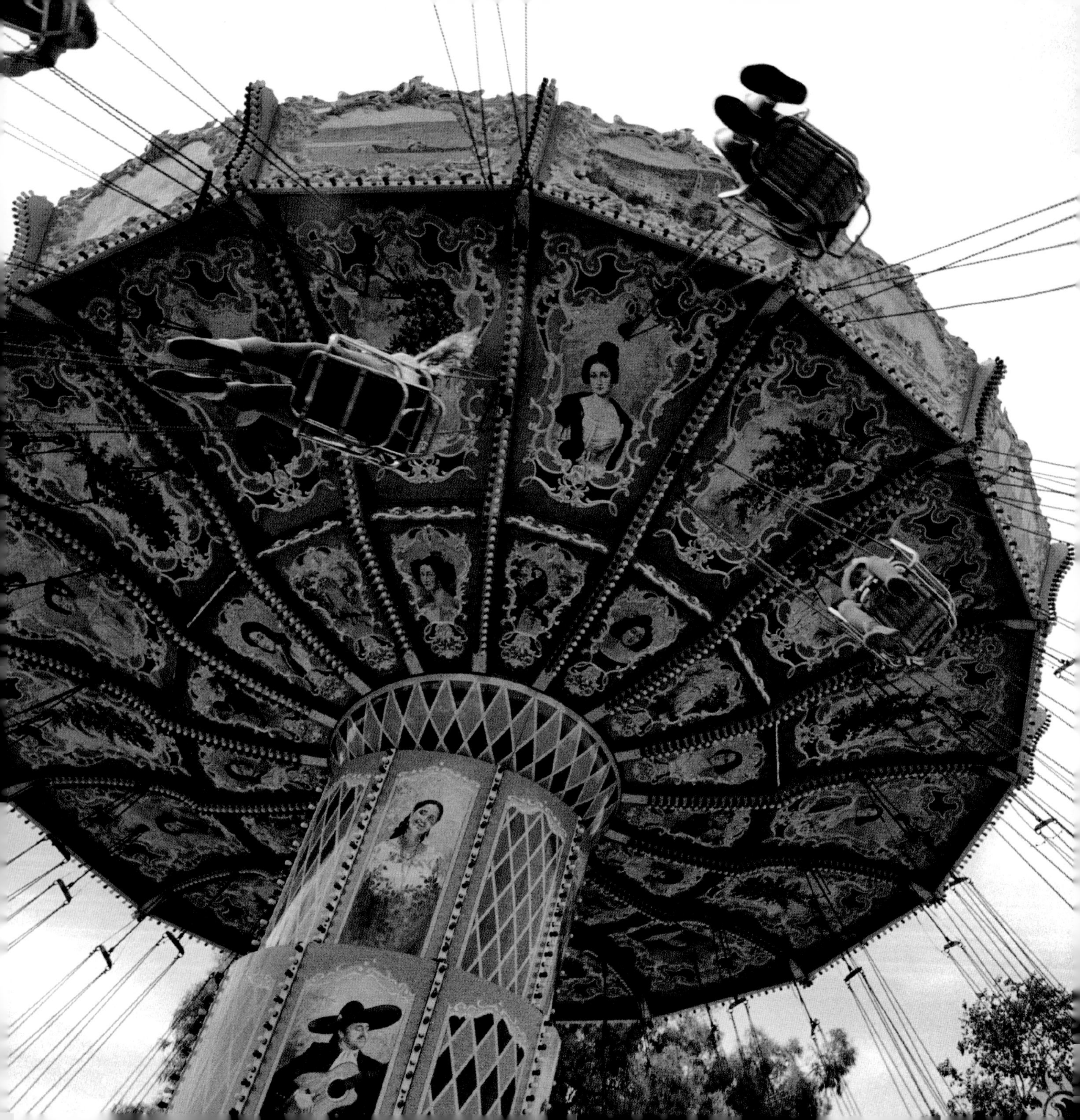

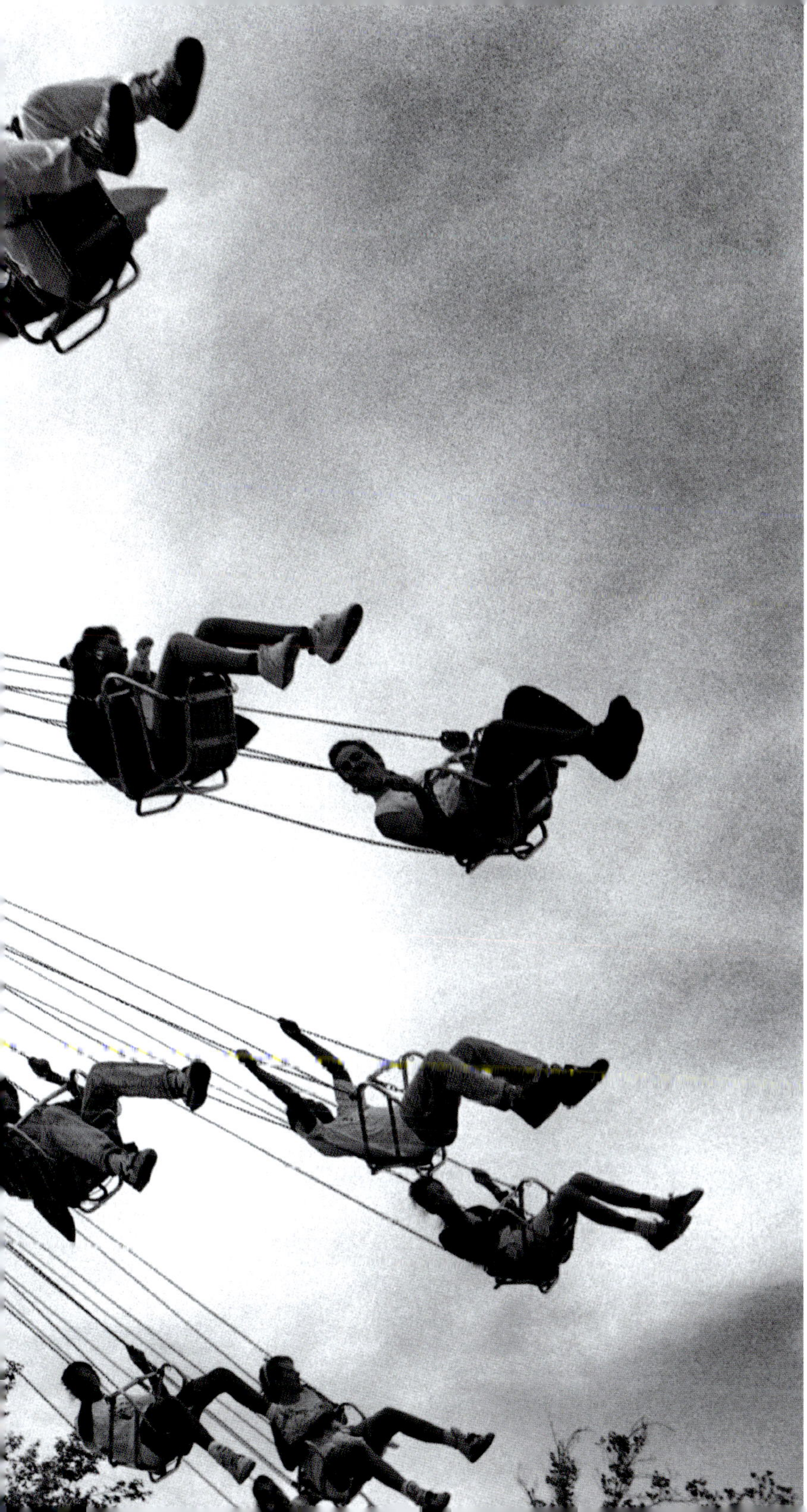

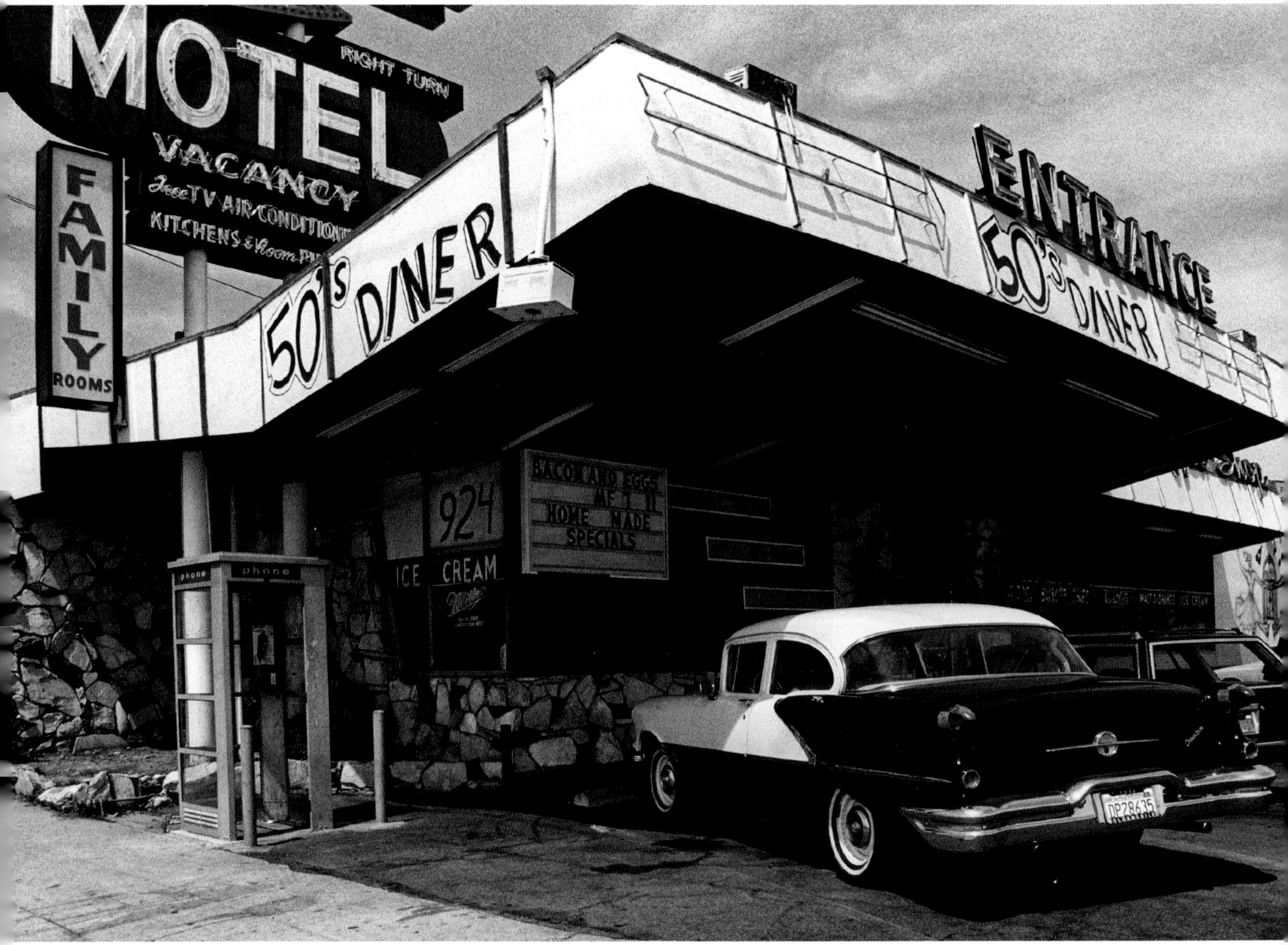
MOTEL
RIGHT TURN
VACANCY
FAMILY
ROOMS
50's DINER
ENTRANCE
50's DINER
BACON AND EGGS
HOME MADE
SPECIALS
924
ICE CREAM
phone
phone

It was this total freedom in conformism that struck me first.

No city is freer than New York. You can do as you like there.

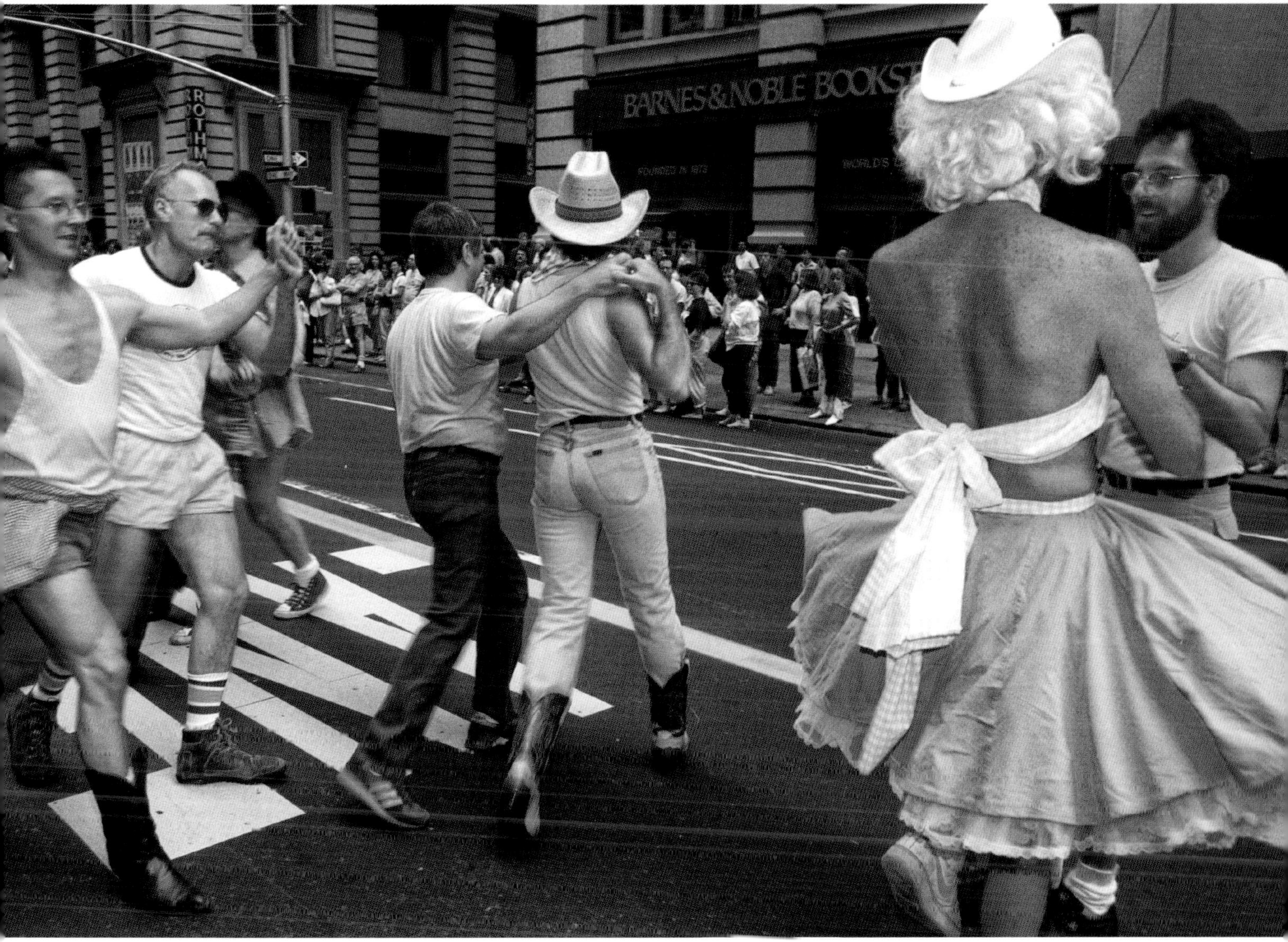
BARNES&NOBLE BOOKST
FOUNDED IN 1873
ROTHM

Public opinion itself keeps order. The few Americans I met seemed conformist out of freedom, depersonalized by rationalism, and they identified universal Reason with their own particular Nation as part of a single creed.

But almost immediately I discovered their profound individualism. This combination of social conformism and individualism is perhaps what a Frenchman will have the greatest difficulty understanding. For us, individualism has retained the old, classical form of 'the individual's struggle against society and, particularly, against the state'. This is not what it means in America. First, the state was for a long time only an administrative body. For some years now, it has tended to play a different role, but this has not changed the Americans' feelings towards it. It is 'their' state, it is the expression of 'their' nation: they have a deep respect and a proprietary love for it.[1]

If you just walk about in New York for a few days, you cannot help but notice the profound link between American conformism and individuality. Taken lengthwise and from side to side, New York, laid flat, is the most conformist city in the world. If you except old Broadway, then from Washington Square not one street curves or runs diagonally. Some ten long parallel furrows run straight from the tip of Manhattan to the Harlem River. These are the avenues and they are crossed by hundreds of smaller furrows that are strictly perpendicular to them.

This grid pattern is New York:

the streets are so alike that they have not been given names;

like soldiers, they have merely been assigned a number.

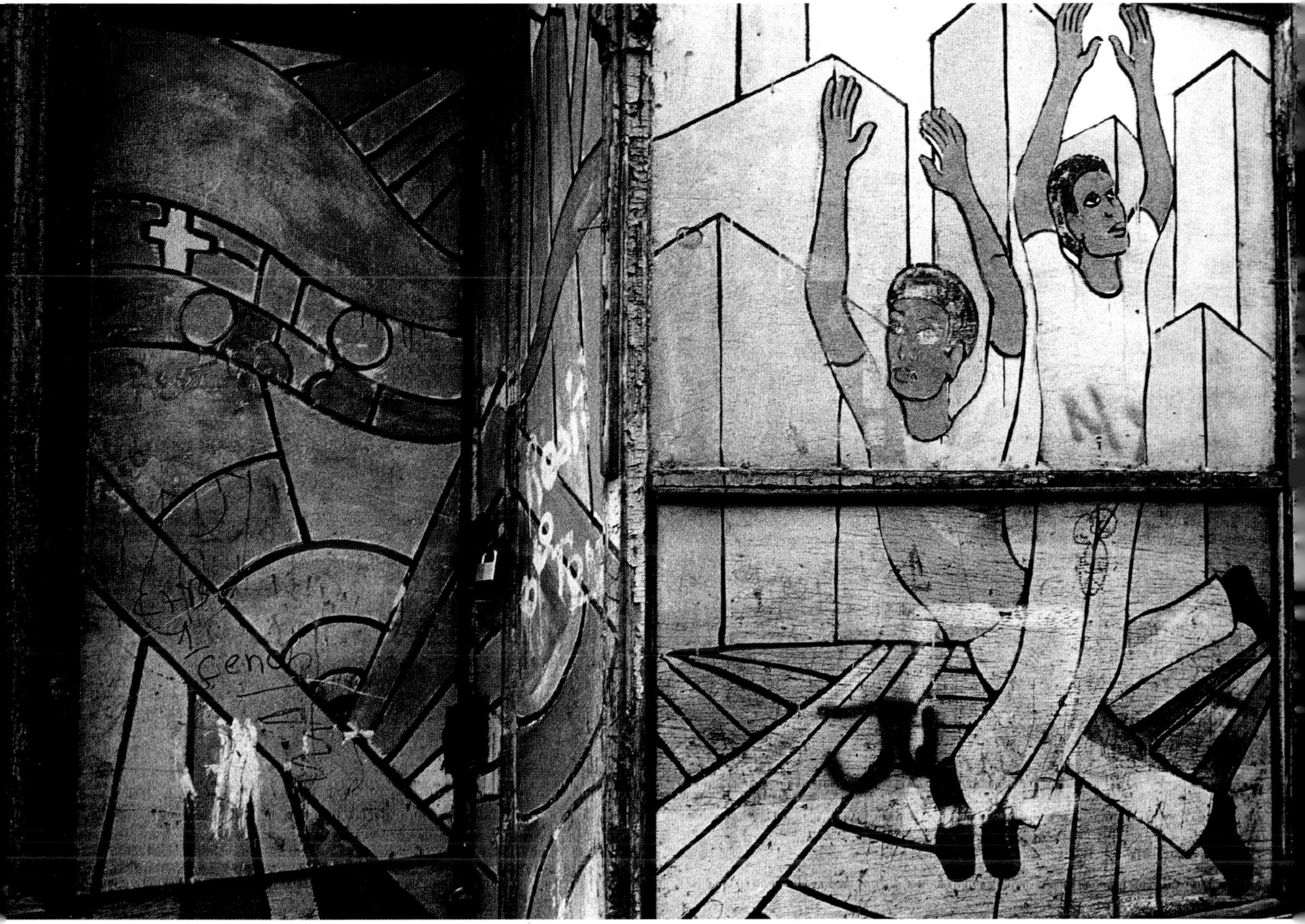

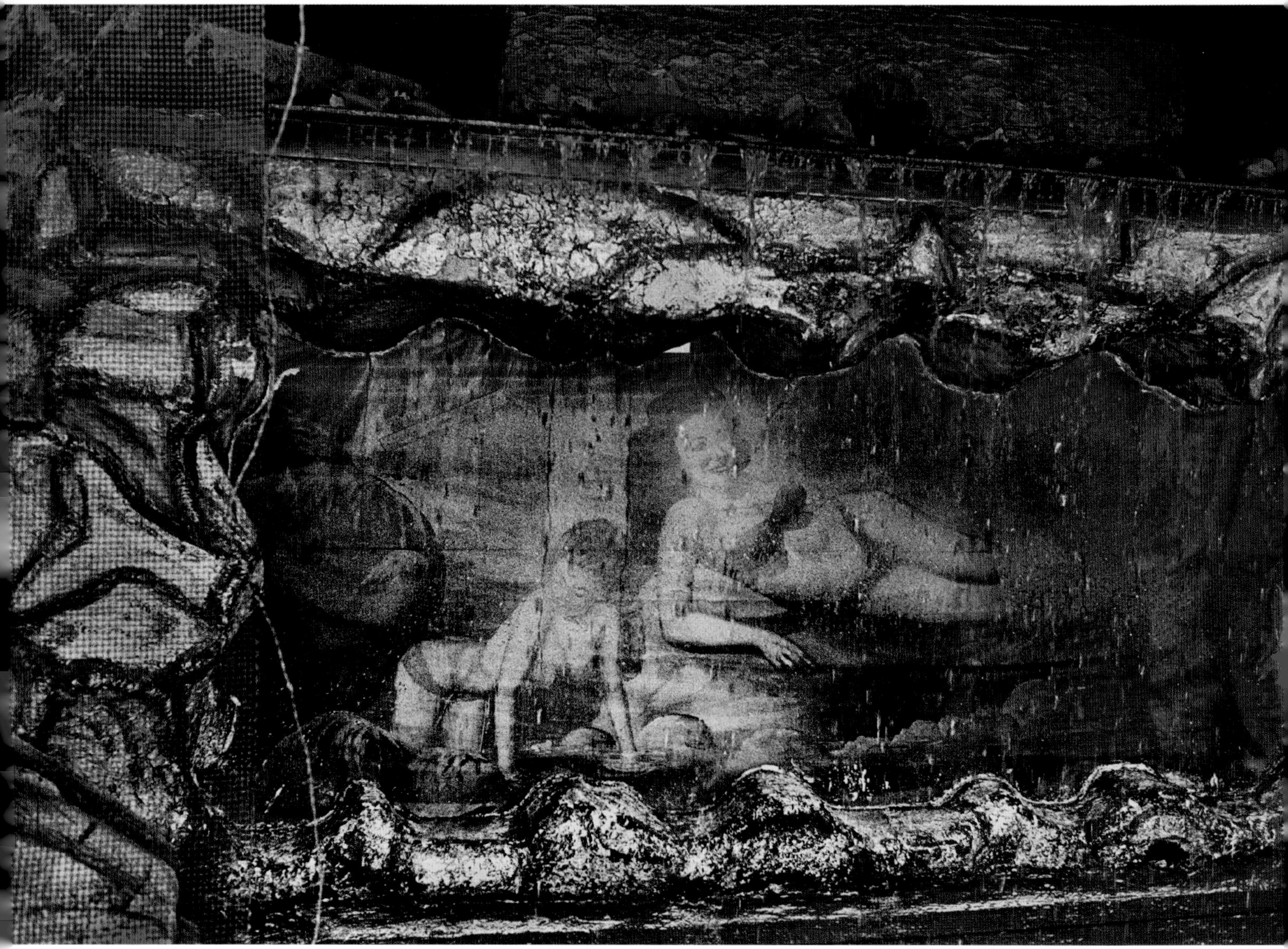

But look up and everything changes.

Viewed in terms of height, New York is the triumph of individualism.

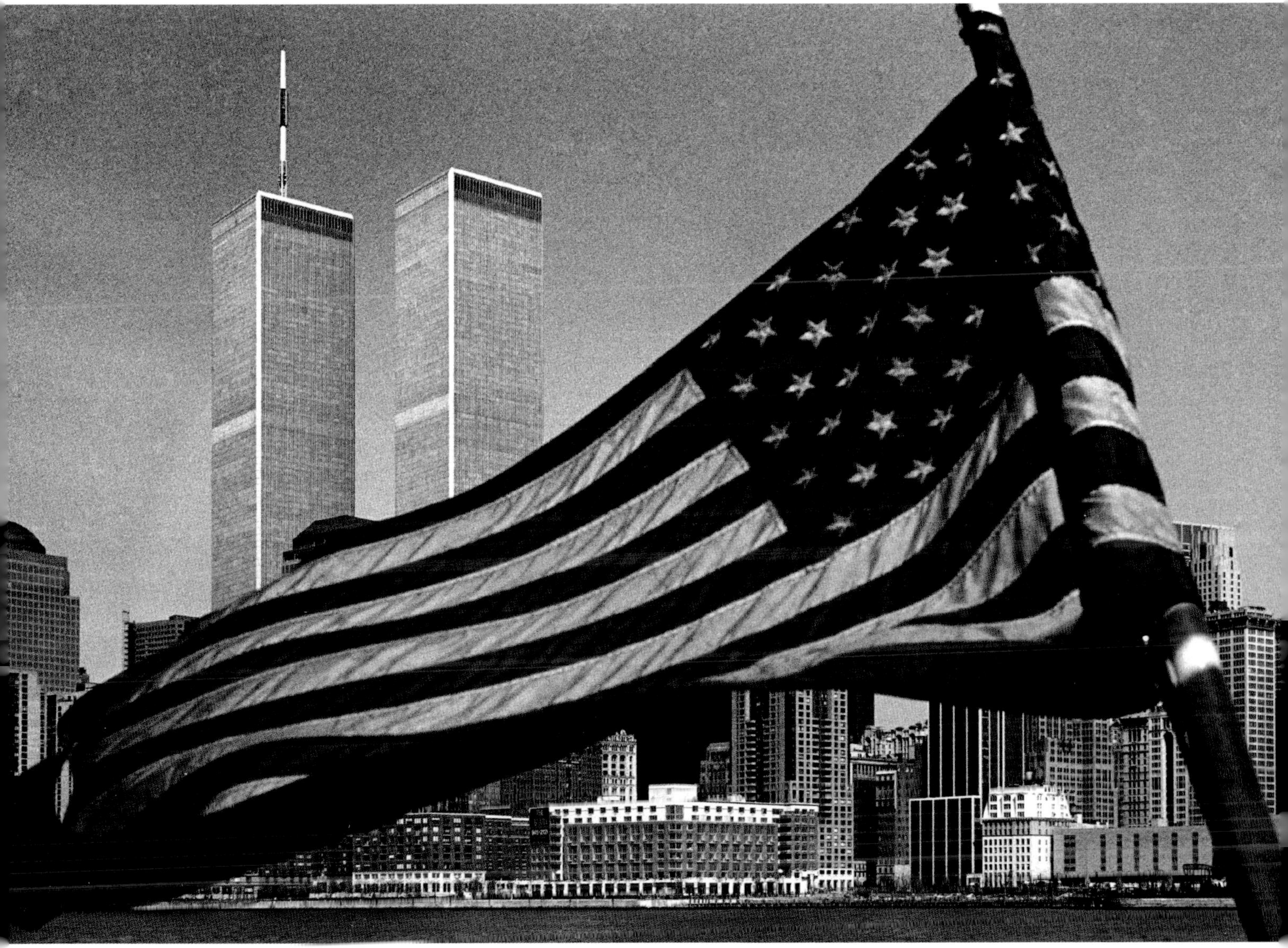

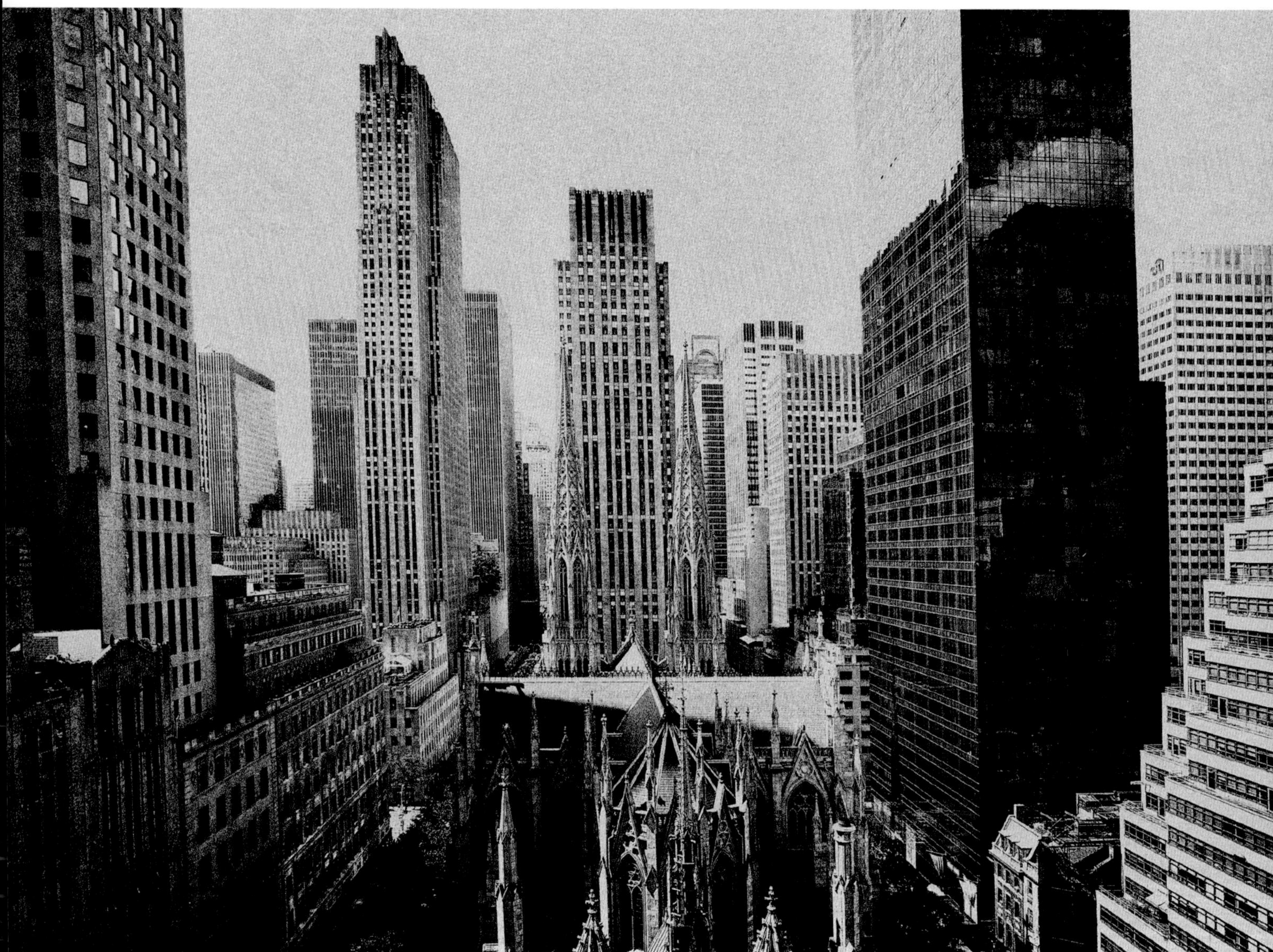

The buildings escape upwards from planning regulations. They have twenty-five, fifty-five or a hundred storeys; they are grey, brown, white, Moorish, medieval, renaissance or modern. On Lower Broadway they press up against each other, dwarfing tiny black churches, and then suddenly

they spread out,

leaving a gaping hole of light between them.

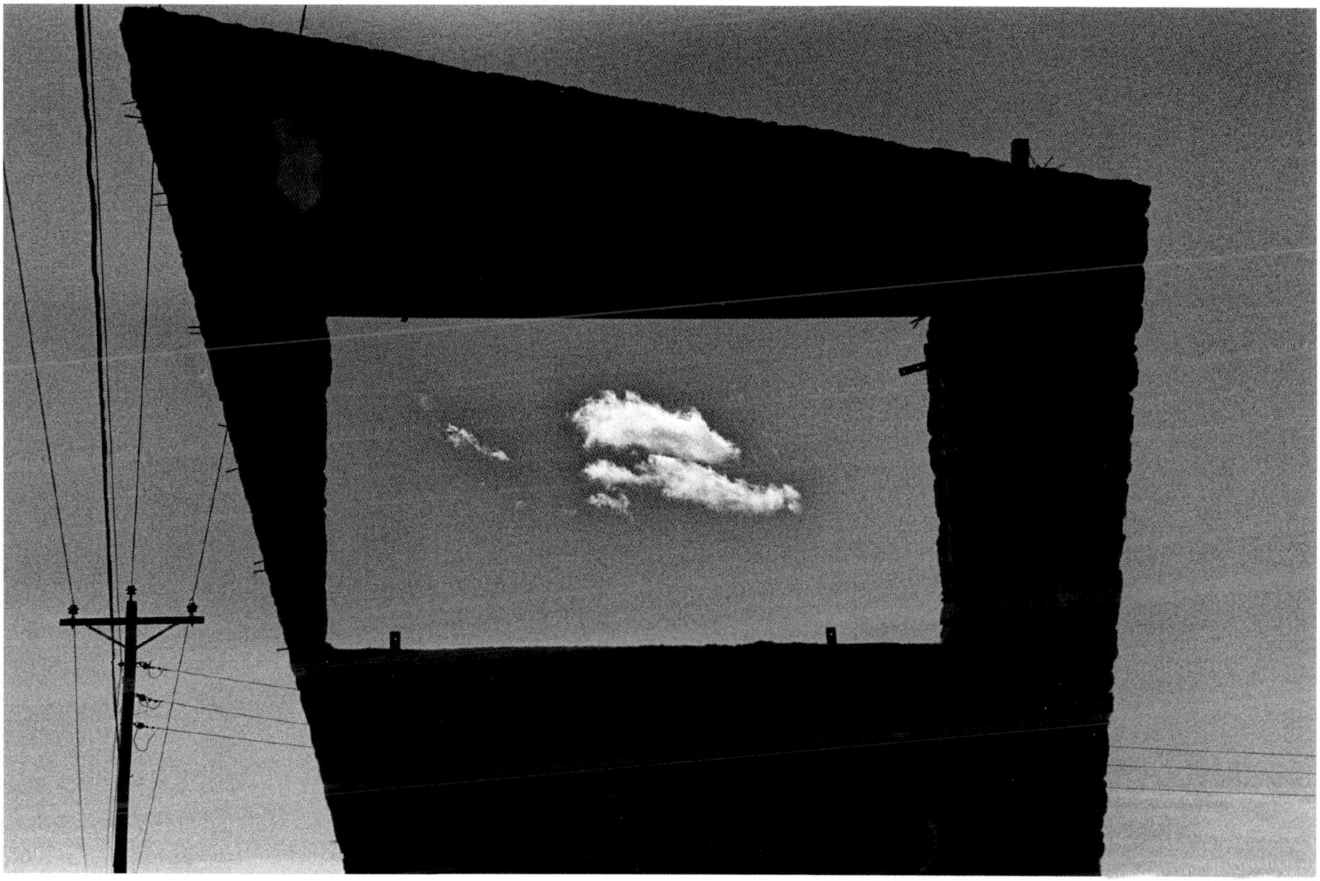

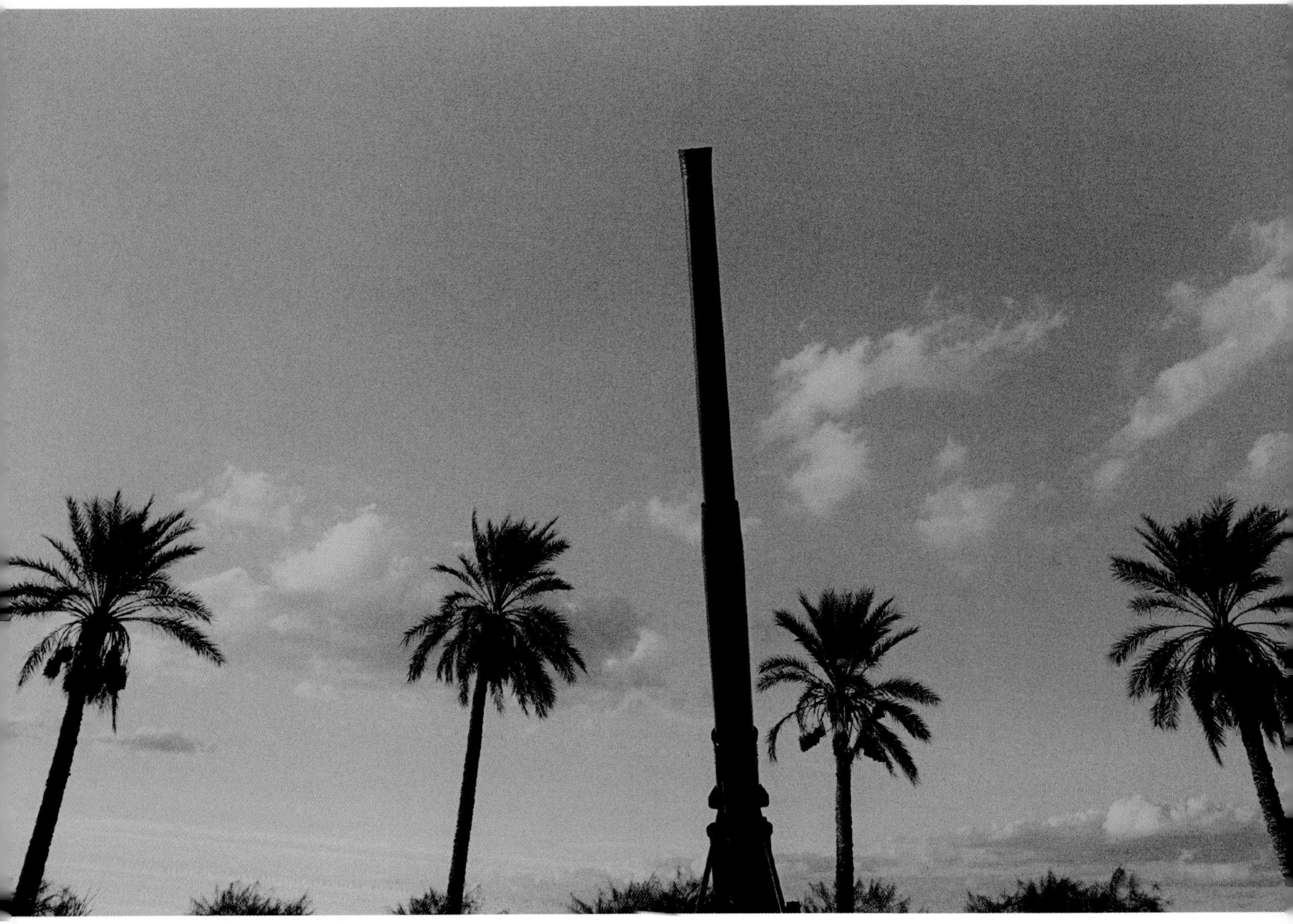

Seen from Brooklyn, they seemed to me to have the solitude and nobility of the clumps of palm trees by the rivers in the Moroccan Souss: clumps of skyscrapers which the eye is always trying to bind together and which always come apart.

So American individualism seemed to me, initially, like a third dimension. In no sense is it opposed to conformism. Indeed, it presupposes it. But within conformism it is a new direction, upwards and downwards.

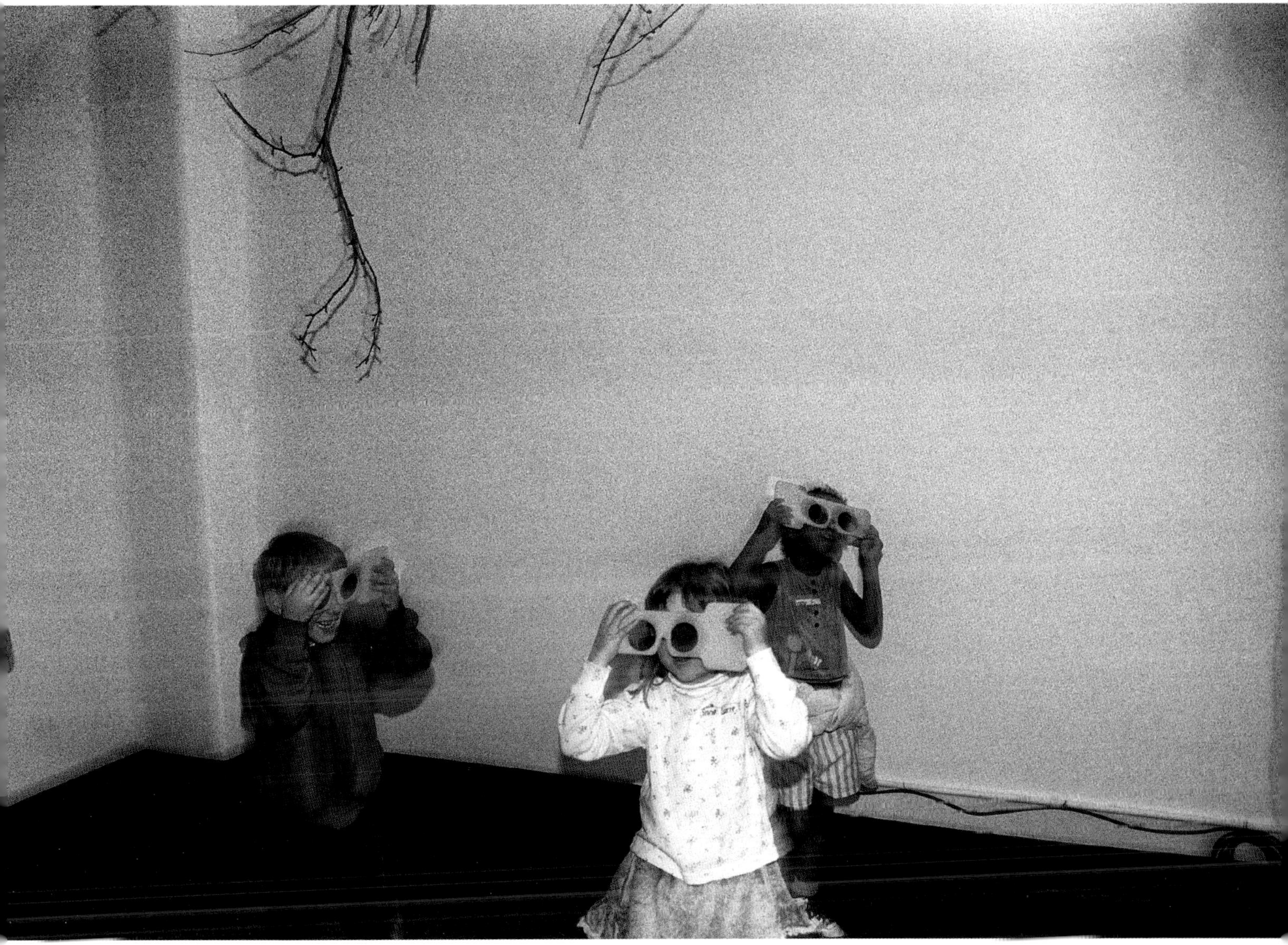

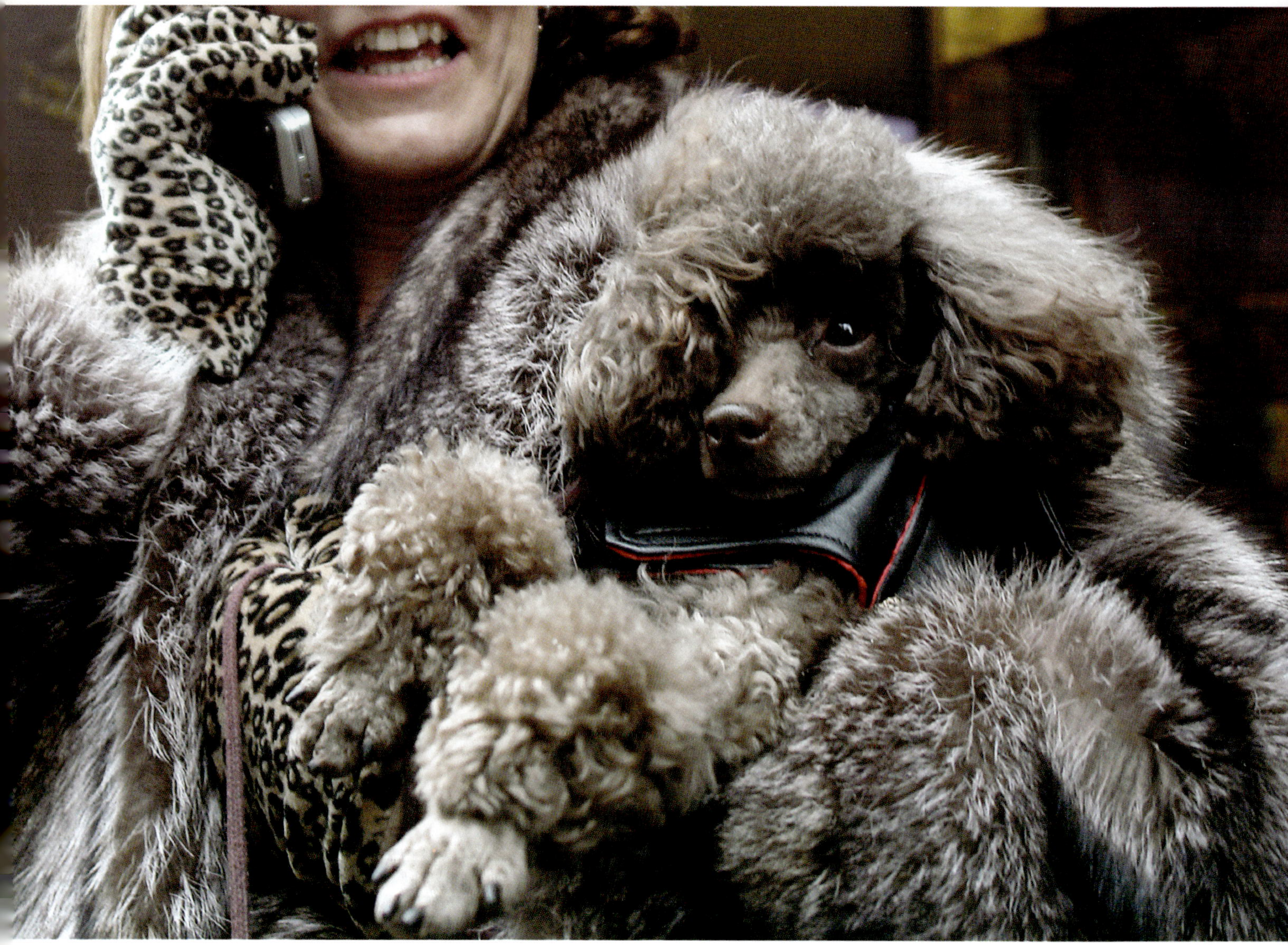

First there is the struggle for existence—

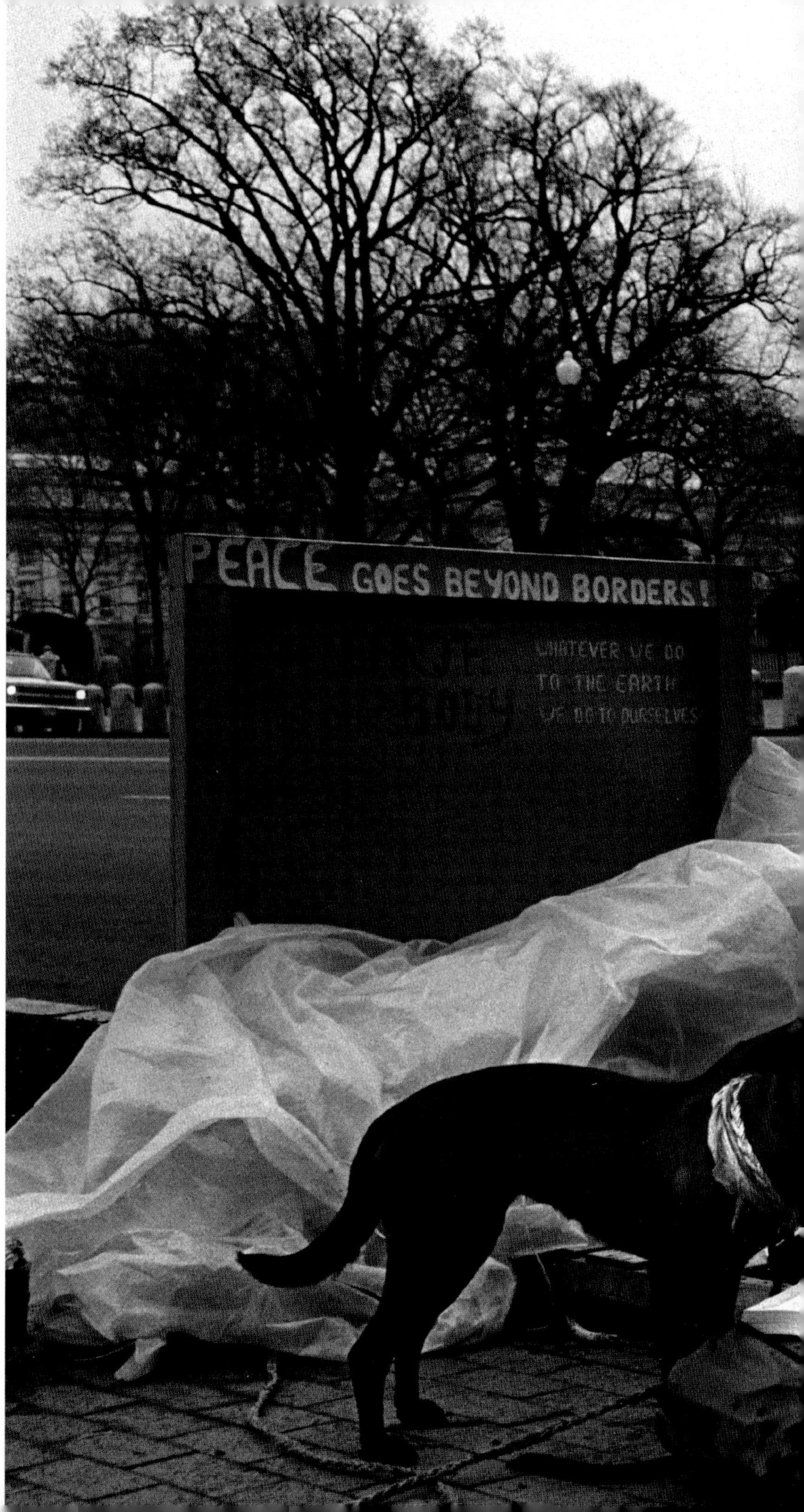
PEACE GOES BEYOND BORDERS!
WHATEVER WE DO
TO THE EARTH
WE DO TO OURSELVES

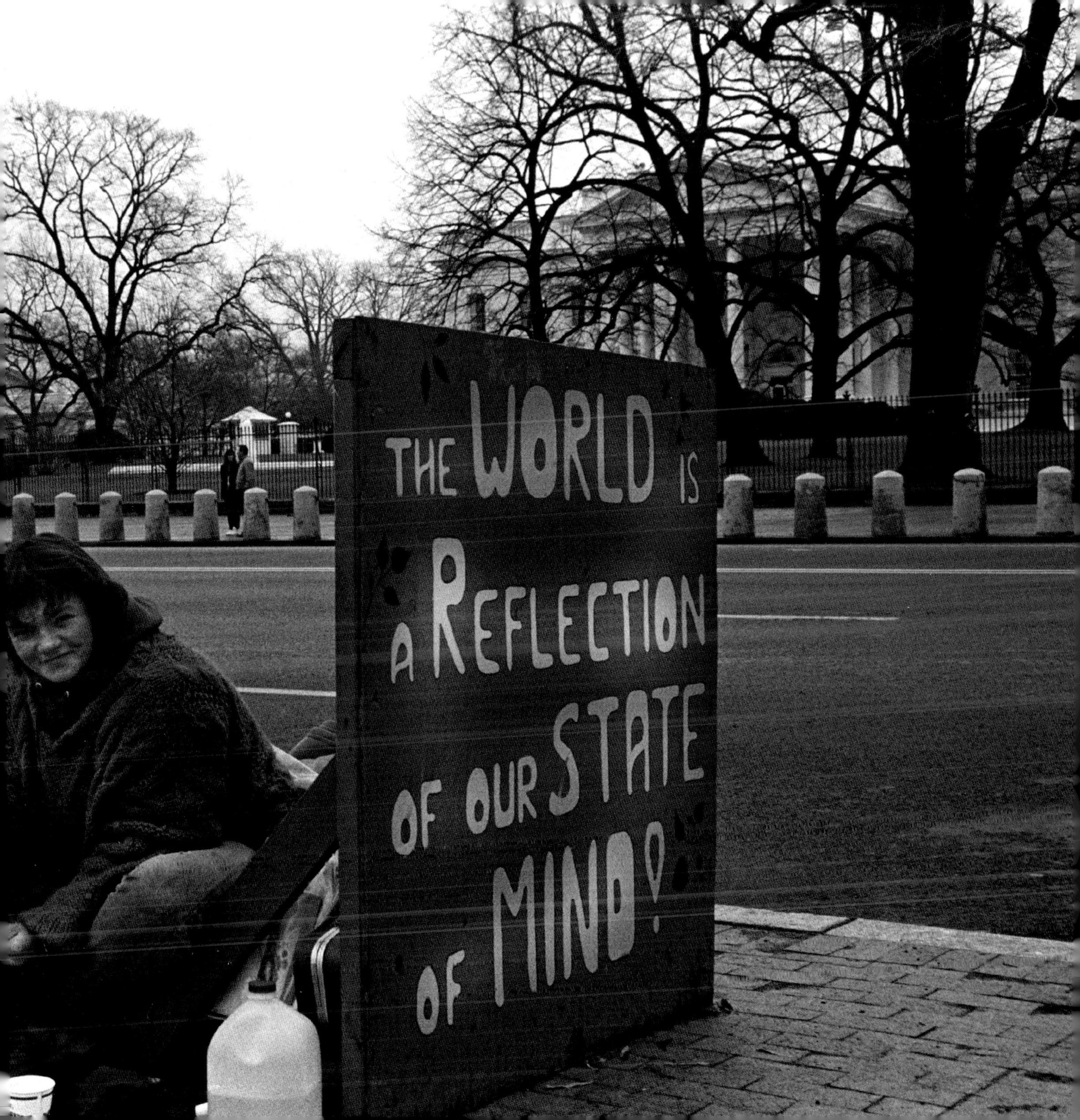
THE WORLD IS
A REFLECTION
OF OUR STATE
OF MIND!

and it is very harsh.

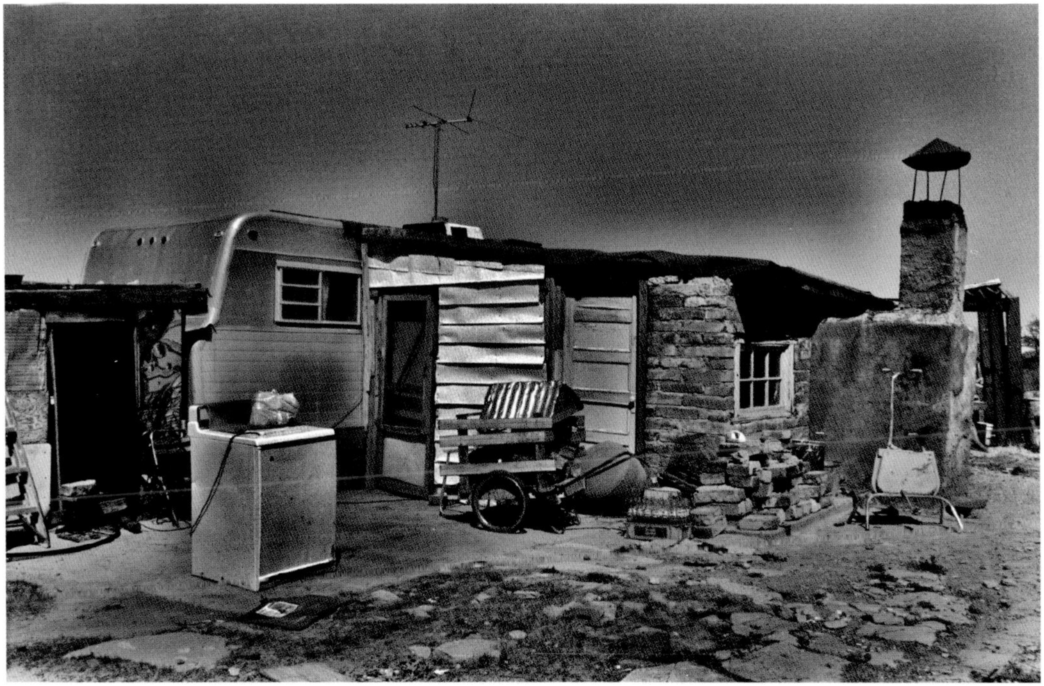

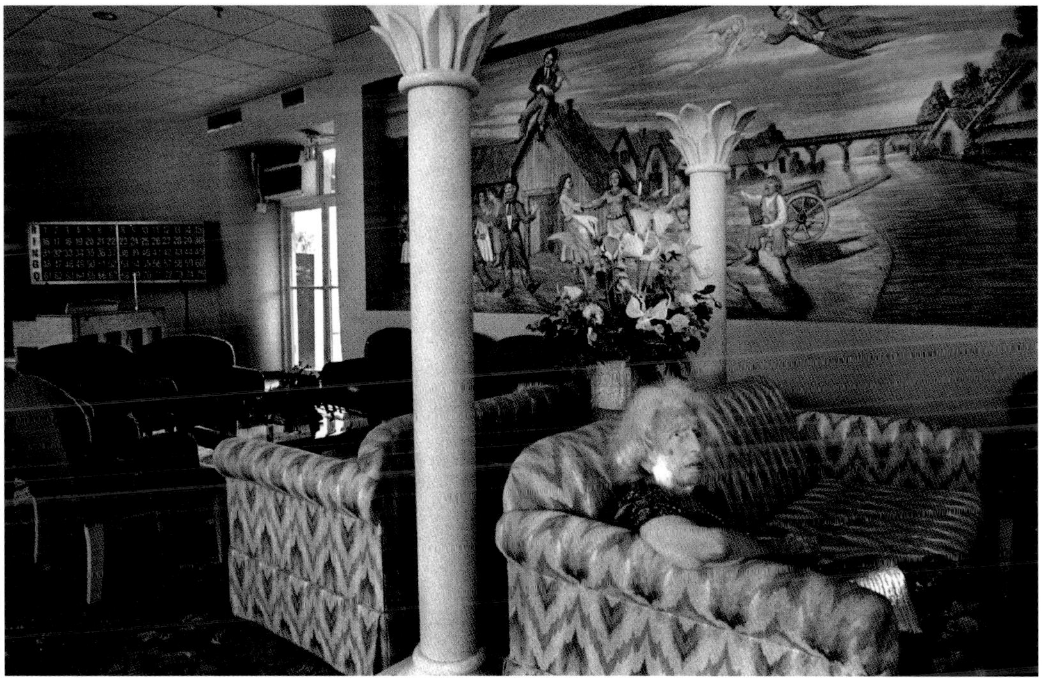

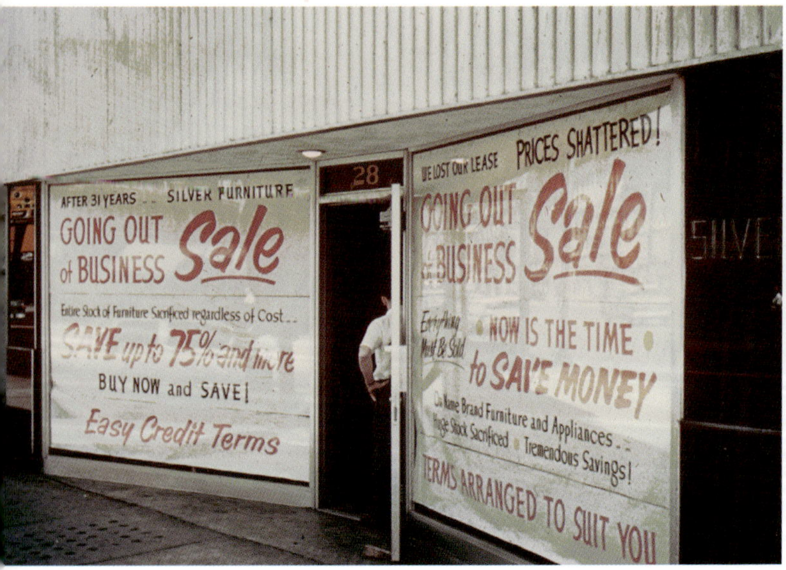
AFTER 31 YEARS ... SILVER FURNITURE
GOING OUT of BUSINESS Sale
Entire Stock of Furniture Sacrificed regardless of Cost ...
SAVE up to 75% and more
BUY NOW and SAVE!
Easy Credit Terms
28
WE LOST OUR LEASE
PRICES SHATTERED!
GOING OUT of BUSINESS Sale
NOW IS THE TIME
to SAVE MONEY
Name Brand Furniture and Appliances ...
Huge Stock Sacrificed
Tremendous Savings!
TERMS ARRANGED TO SUIT YOU

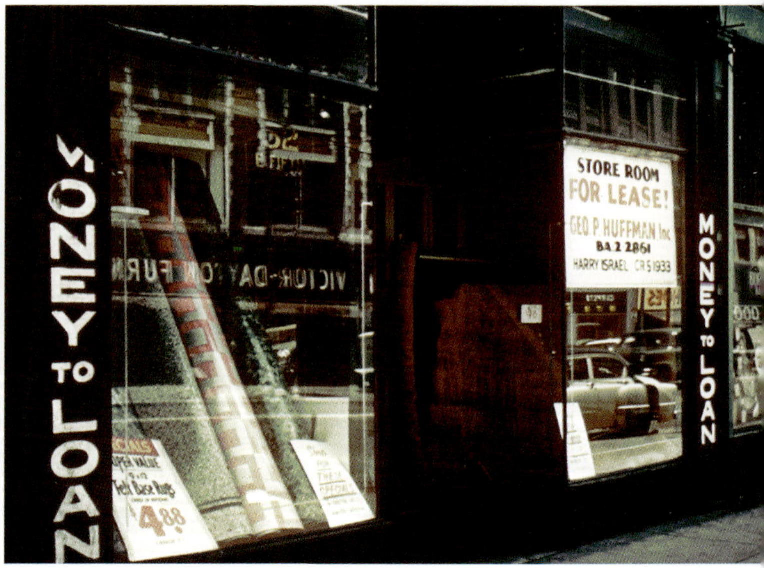
MONEY TO LOAN
STORE ROOM
FOR LEASE!
GEO P HUFFMAN Inc
BA 2 2861
HARRY ISRAEL CR 5 1933
MONEY TO LOAN

Every individual wants to succeed—that is to say, to make money. But we should not see this as greed, nor even as a taste for luxury. It seems to me that in the US, money is merely the necessary, but symbolic, token of success.

You must succeed, because success proves your moral virtue and intelligence, and because it indicates that you enjoy divine protection.

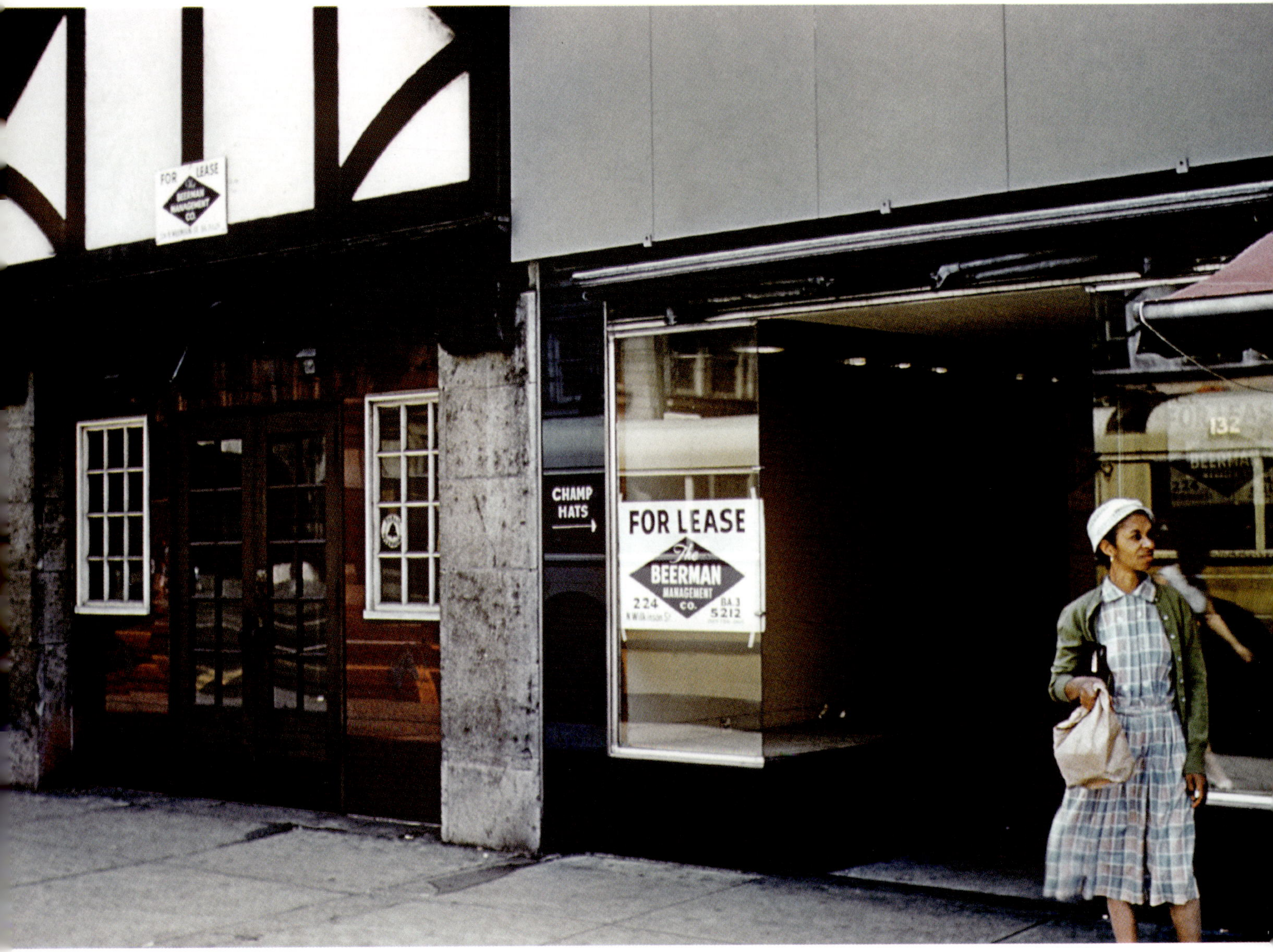
FOR LEASE
The BEERMAN MANAGEMENT CO.
CHAMP HATS
FOR LEASE
The BEERMAN MANAGEMENT CO.
224
N Wilkinson St.
BA 3
5212
132

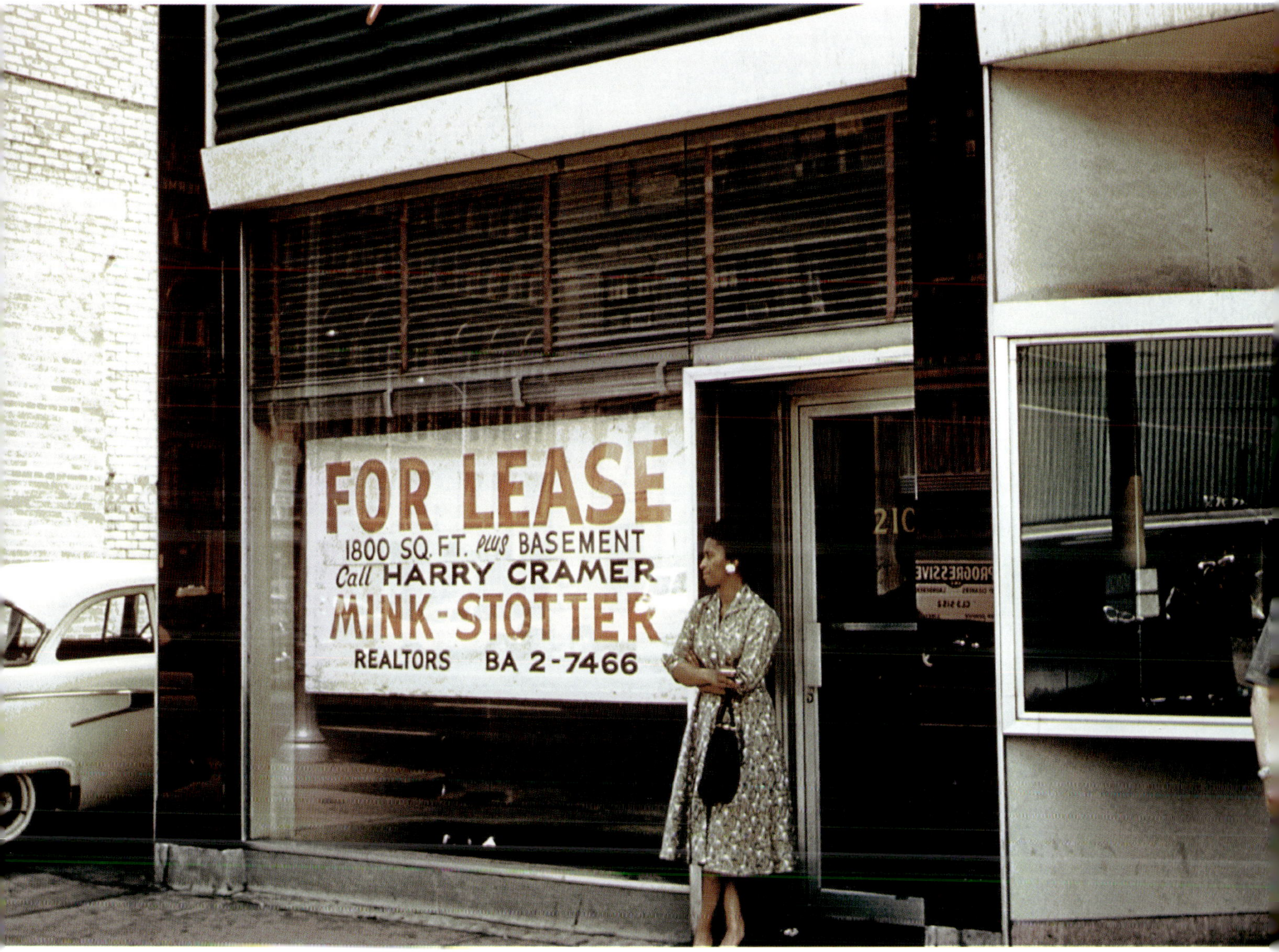
FOR LEASE
1800 SQ. FT. PLUS BASEMENT
Call HARRY CRAMER
MINK-STOTTER
REALTORS BA 2-7466

And you must succeed because only then can you stand out from the crowd as a person.

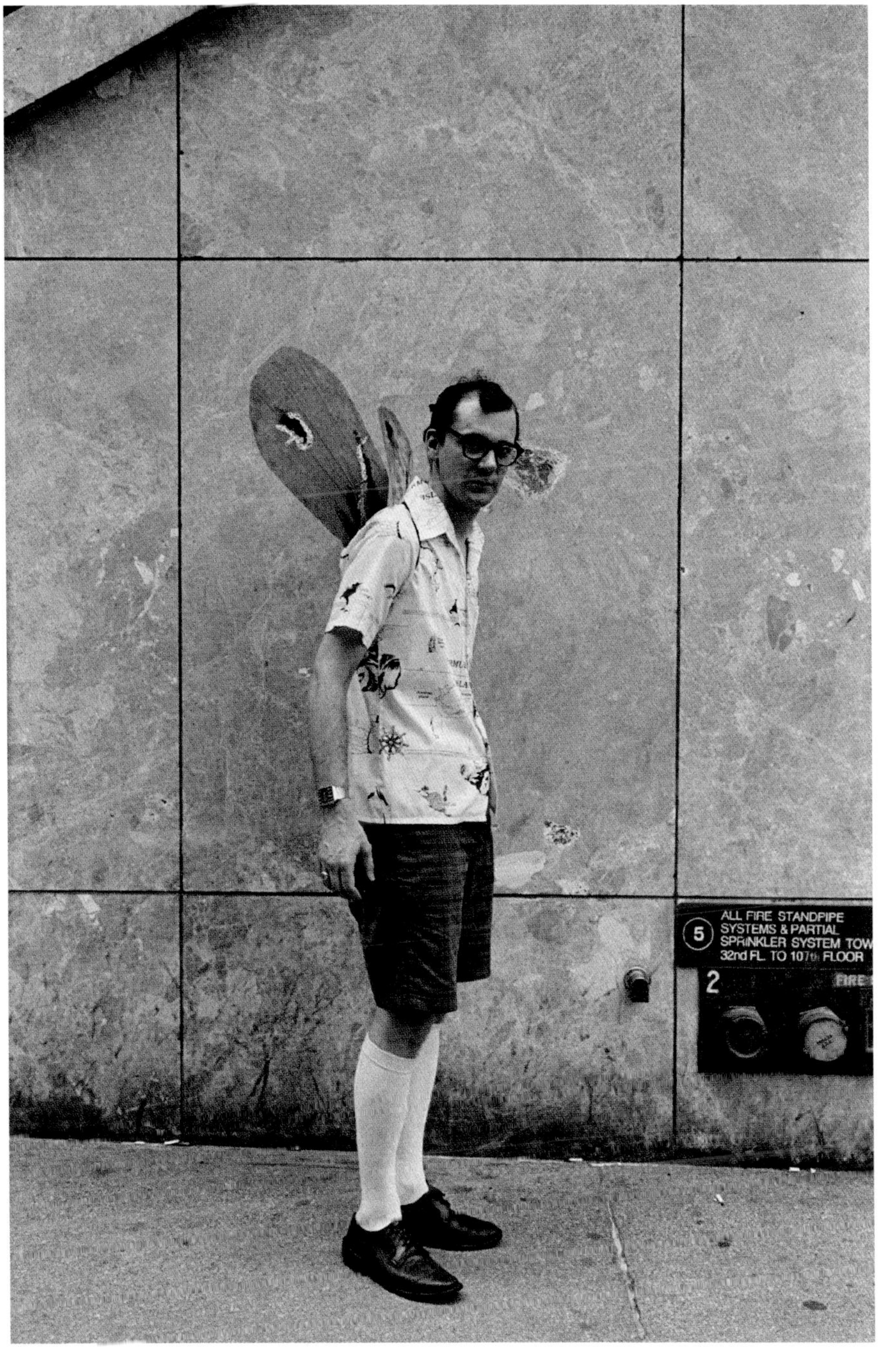
ALL FIRE STANDPIPE
SYSTEMS & PARTIAL
SPRINKLER SYSTEM TOW
32nd FL. TO 107th FLOOR

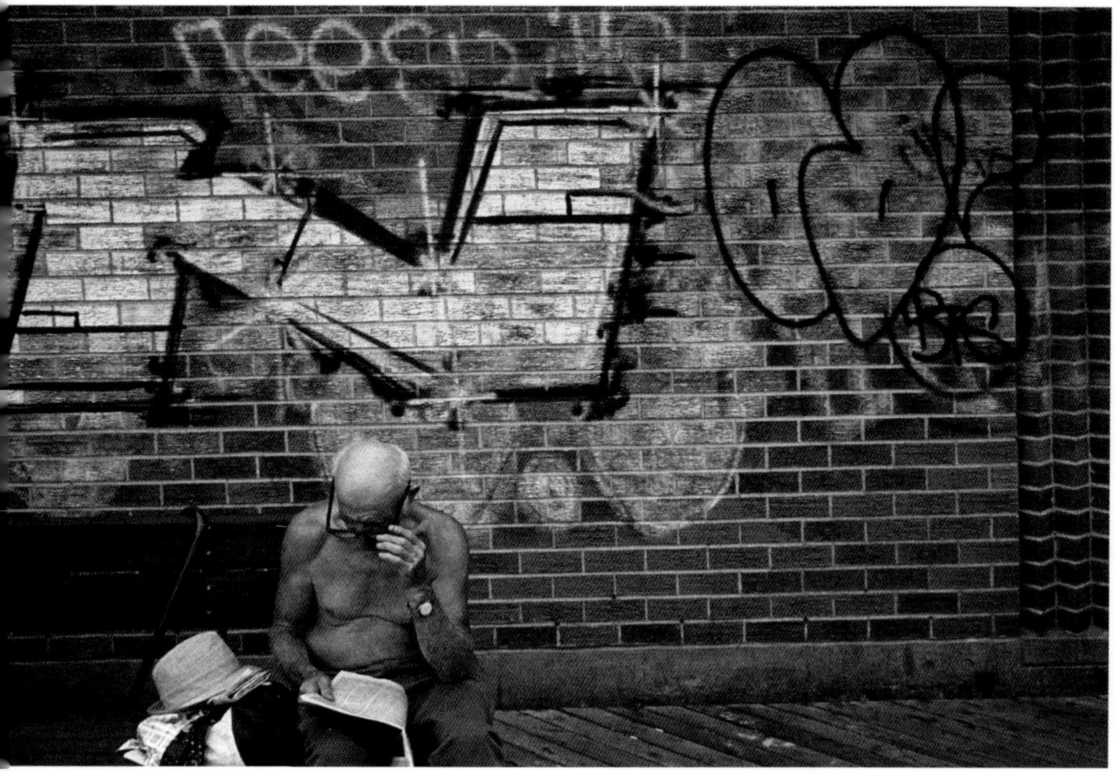

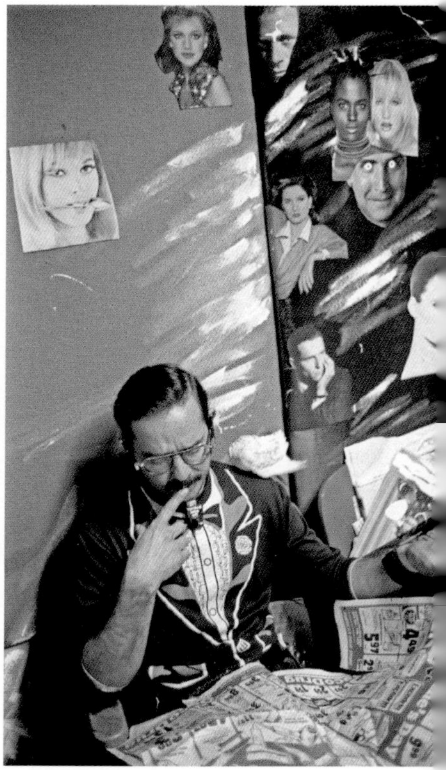

Take the American newspapers. Until you are a success, there is no point hoping that your articles will be published in the form in which you submitted them. They will be cut and pruned. But if you have a name that makes money, all that changes. What you write will go through without editing. You have acquired the right to be yourself.

It is the same in the theatre. A lady very well versed in French literature and well known in publishing circles asked me if I would like to have a play put on in the States. I replied that I would be happy to, if the directors were not, as I had been told, in the habit of reworking the scripts submitted to them. She seemed most surprised and said, 'If they don't do it, who will? What you wrote is meant to be read. But they have to work on it, so that it can be understood.'[2]

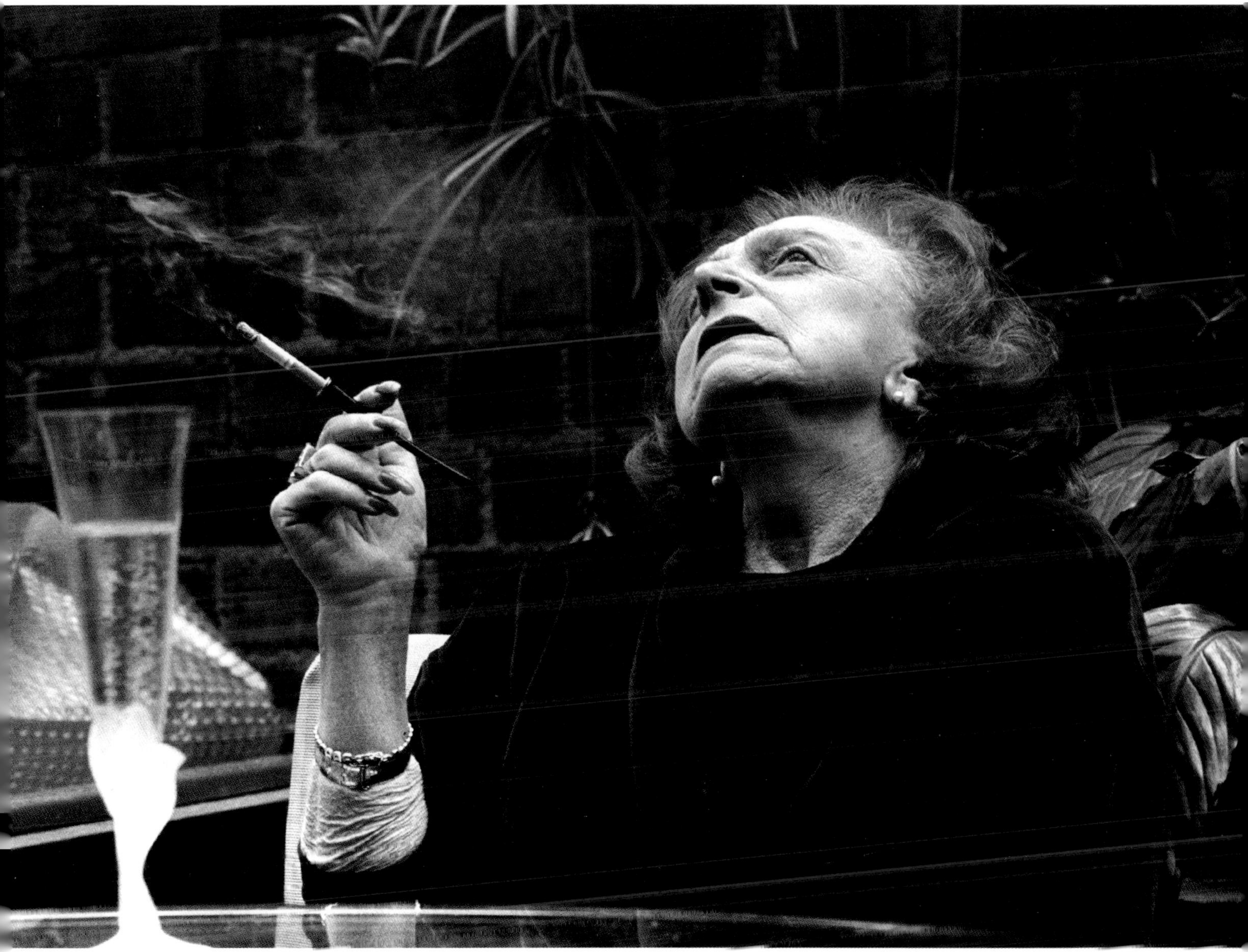

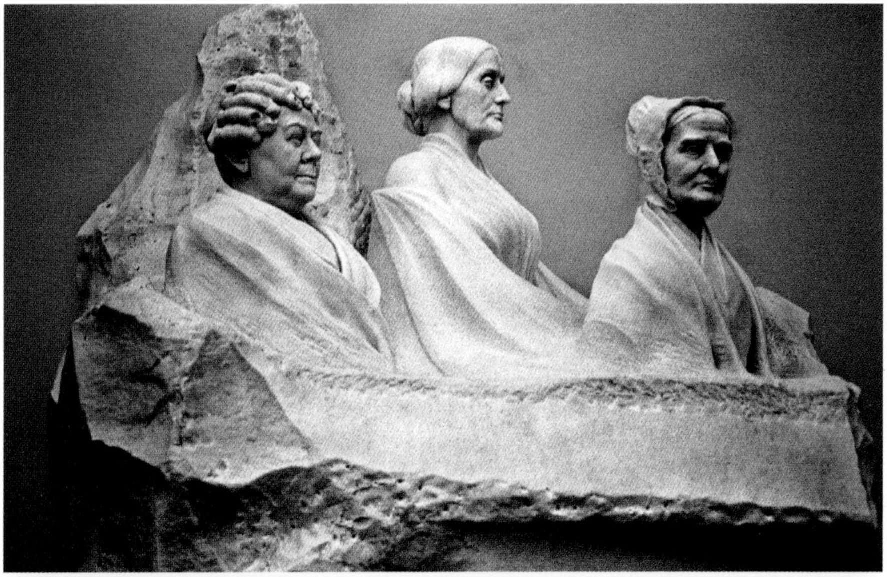

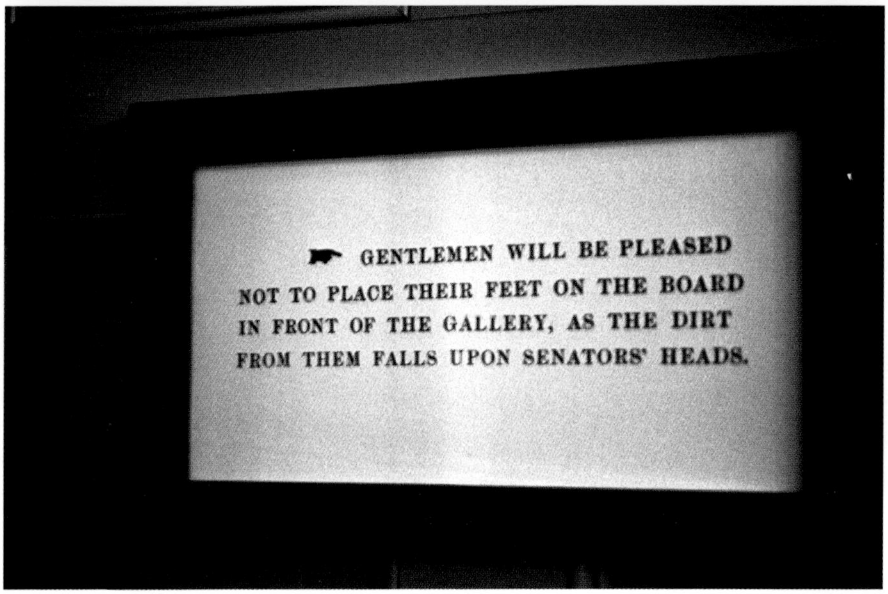
GENTLEMEN WILL BE PLEASED
NOT TO PLACE THEIR FEET ON THE BOARD
IN FRONT OF THE GALLERY, AS THE DIRT
FROM THEM FALLS UPON SENATORS' HEADS.

So, individualism in America is, above all, each person's passionate aspiration, in the struggle for existence, to the state of individual. There are individuals in America the way there are skyscrapers. There's Ford, there's Rockefeller, there's Hemingway, there's Roosevelt: they are models and examples.

In this sense, the office blocks are votive offerings to success. Behind the Statue of Liberty, they are like the statues of a man or an enterprise that have risen above the others. They are huge publicity ventures, built by individuals or groups to demonstrate their financial triumph. Their owners occupy only a small part of the premises and let out the rest. I was not mistaken, then, in taking them to symbolize New York individualism. They quite simply mark the fact that in the United States individuality is something to be achieved. It is no doubt for this reason that New Yorkers seemed to me so passionately attached to a free-market economy.

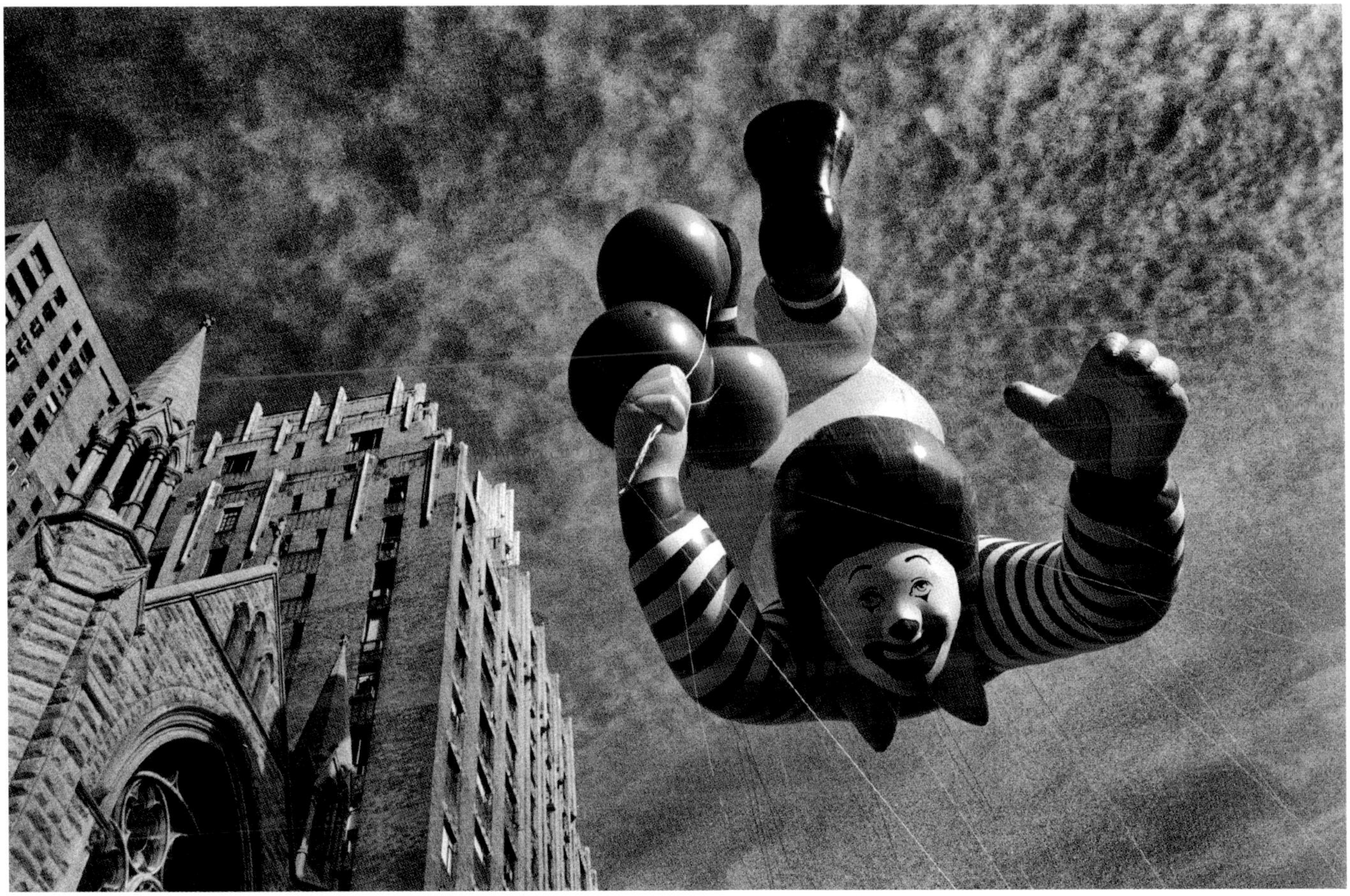

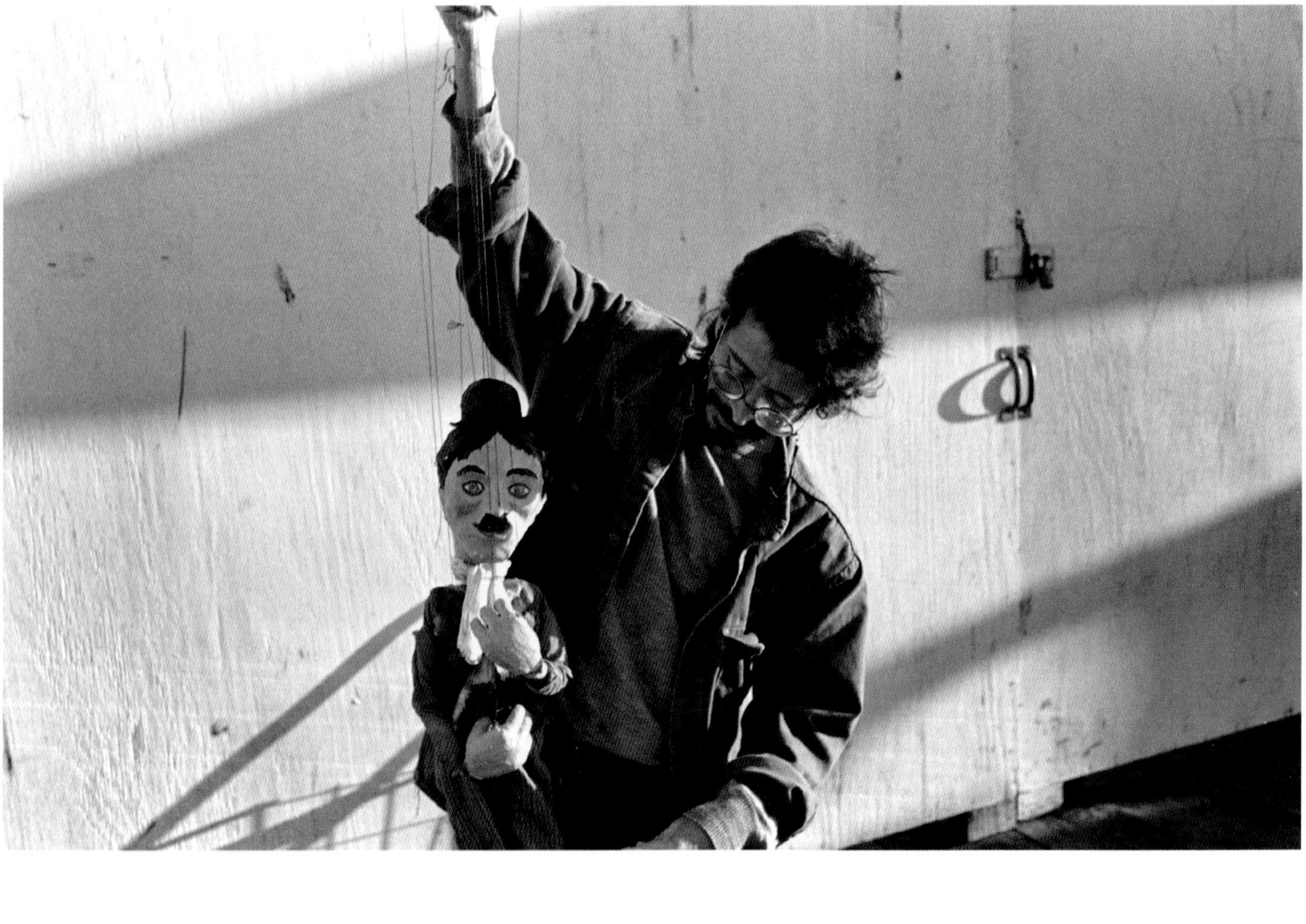

Yet everyone knows the power of the trusts in the US, which represents, all in all, another form of command economy. But the New Yorker hasn't forgotten the day when a man could earn a fortune off his own bat. What he finds distasteful in the command economy is bureaucracy. So, rather paradoxically, this man who allows himself to be led so obediently by the nose in his public and private life is intransigent when it comes to his job. This he regards as the sphere of his independence, initiative and personal dignity.

For everything else, there are the 'associations'. In 1930, there were more than a hundred and fifty headquarters of associations and groups in Washington. I shall mention just one of them, the Foreign Policy Association.

On some seventeenth floor, 'over a cup of tea', we met some of those tall, grey-haired women, who have made up a majority in these associations since the war began; they are amiable but rather cold, and as intelligent as men. They told us how in 1917 a number of people, firmly convinced that the United States was entering the war without knowing anything of foreign affairs, had decided to devote their free time to providing the country with the information it lacked.

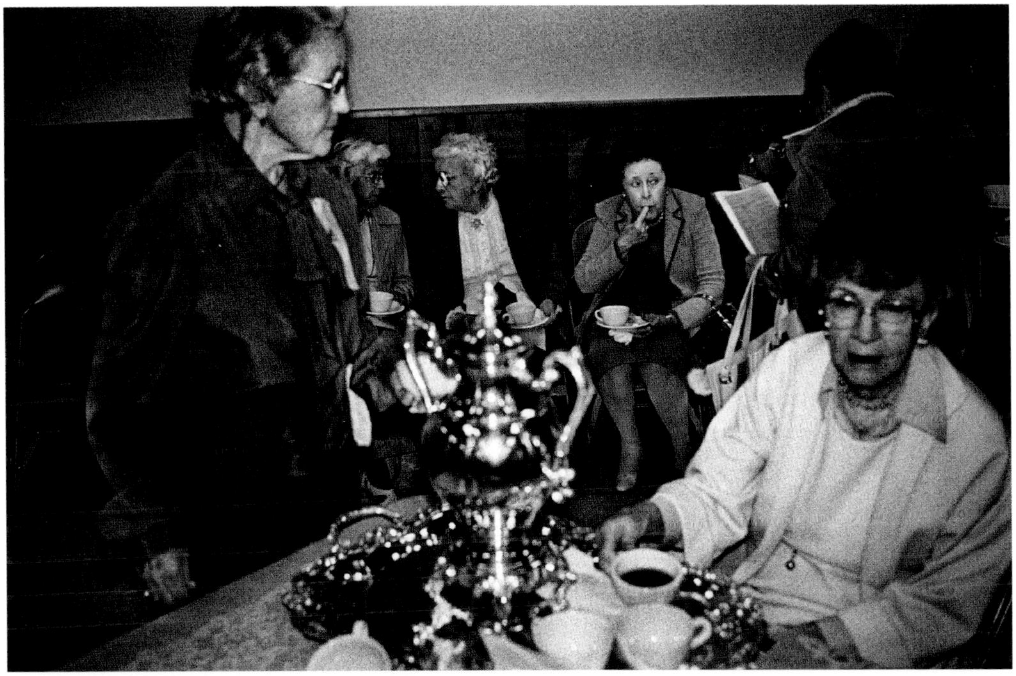

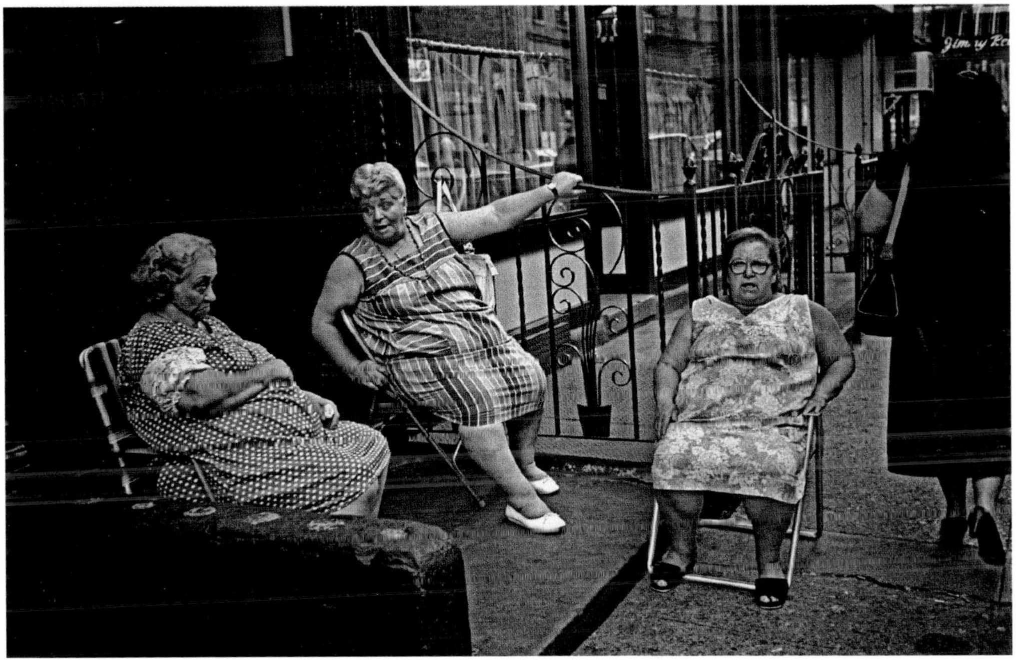

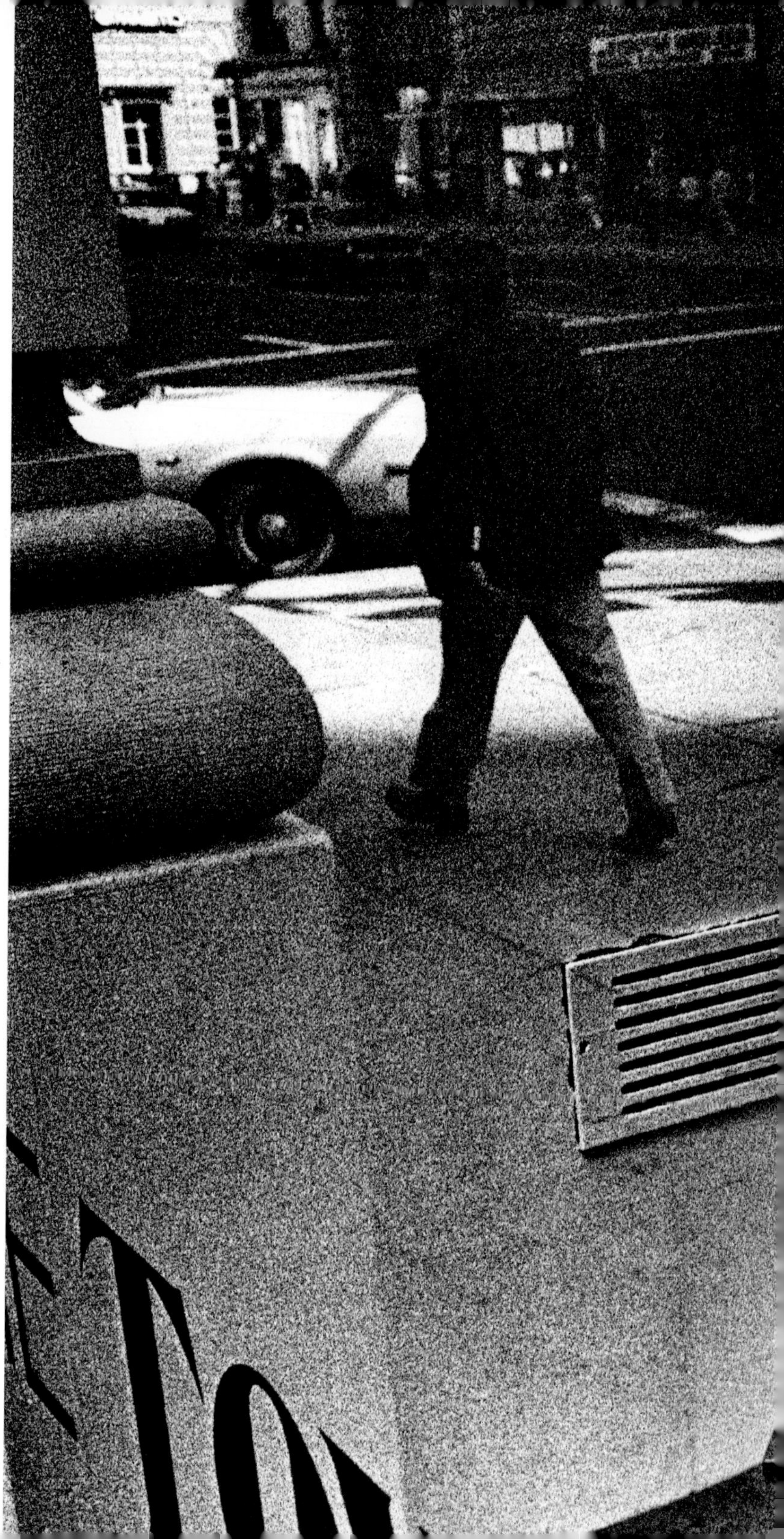

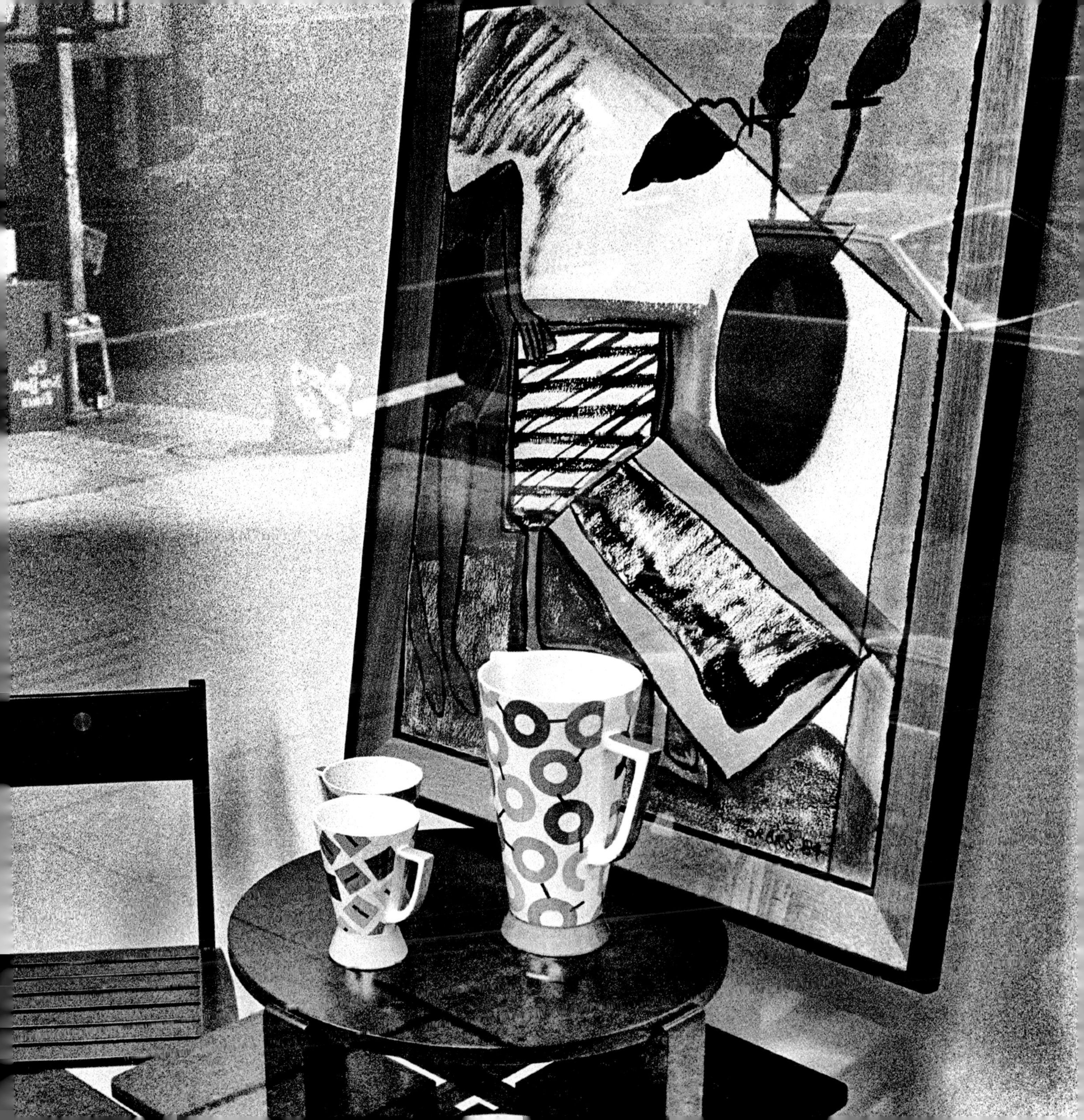

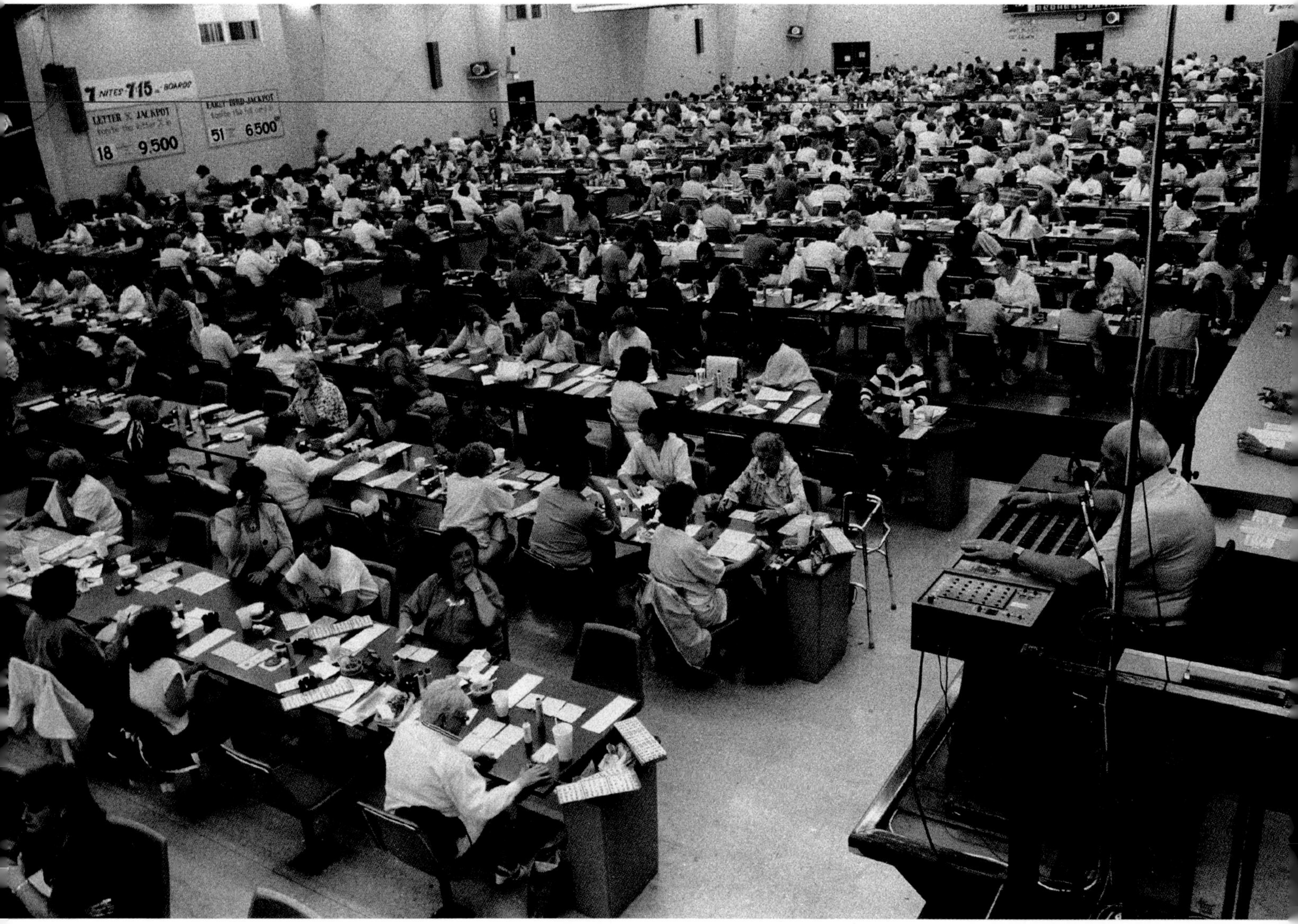
LETTER X JACKPOT
18
9,500
EARLY BIRD JACKPOT
51
6500

The organization has twenty-six thousand members today, with three hundred branches in the various states. It provides documentation to more than five hundred newspapers. Politicians consult its publications. It has, indeed, given up on informing the general public: it now informs the informers (scholars, teachers, priests and journalists). Every week it publishes a bulletin with a study of an international question and commentary on events in Washington and once a fortnight it sends documentation to the newspapers which they reprint in whole or in part.

Can one imagine in the France of 1939 an association of this kind providing Bonnet or Daladier with information and sending its bulletins to Maurras for inclusion in *Action française* and to Cachin for *L'Humanité* ?

What struck me most forcefully were our hostess' last words: 'The point,' she said, 'is that we protect the individual. Outside of the associations a man is alone; in the associations he is a person; and he protects himself against each of them by belonging to several.'

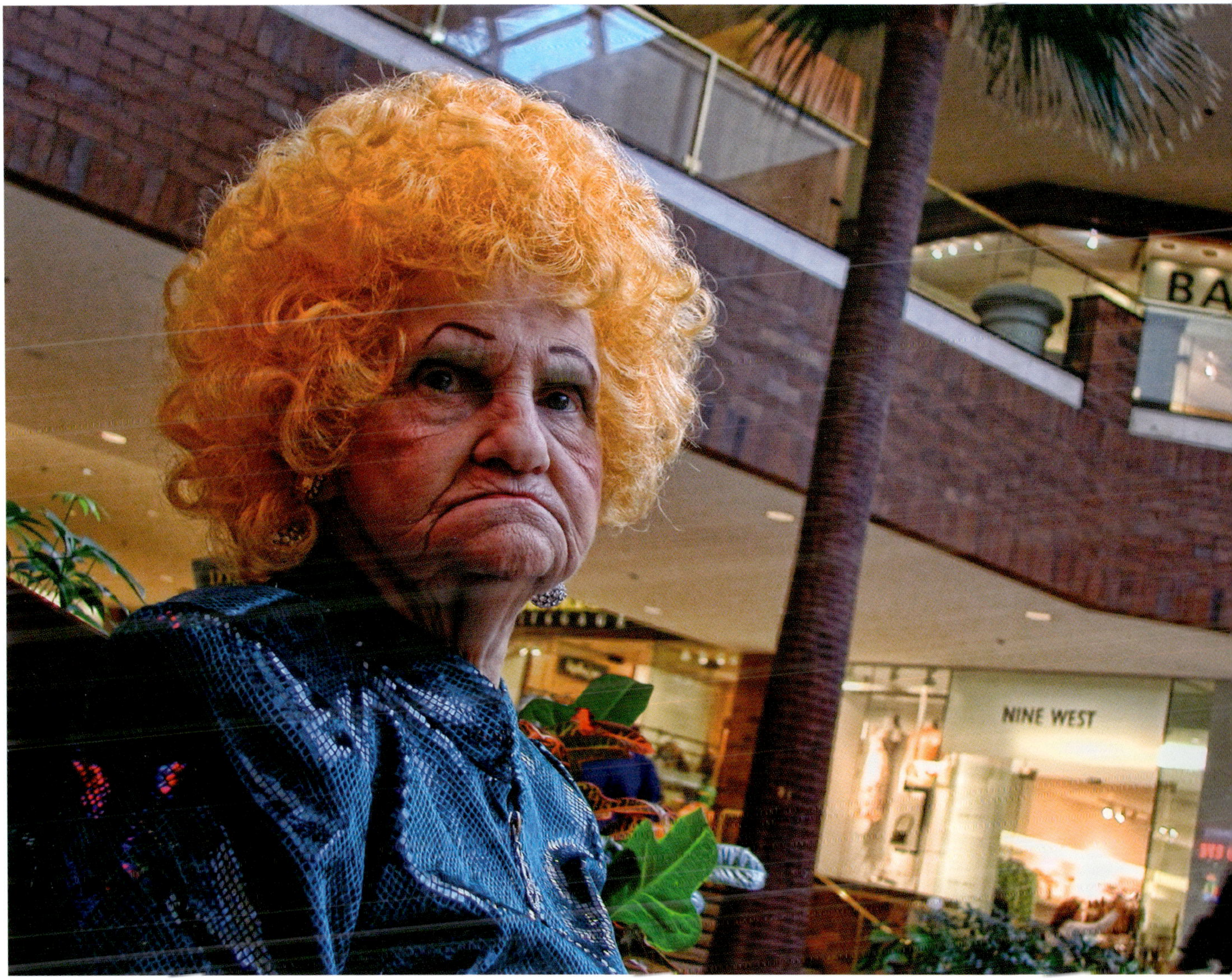
NINE WEST

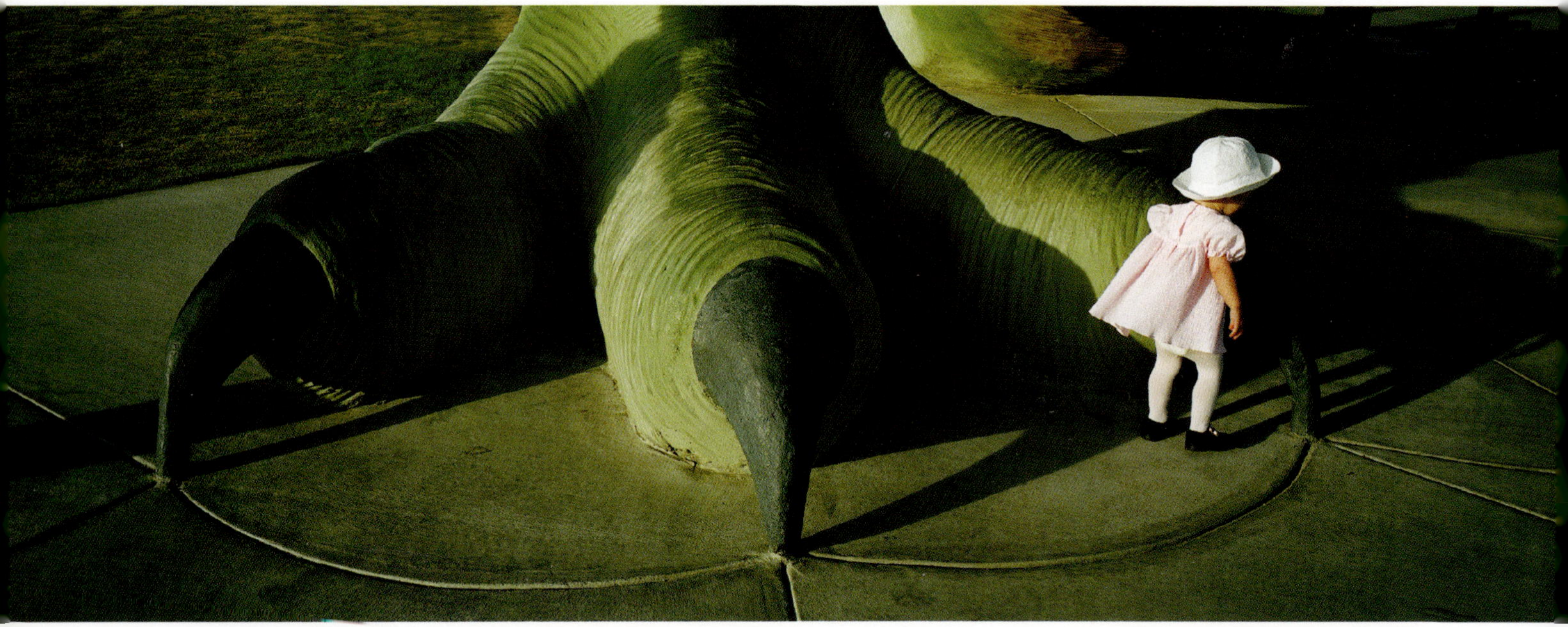

You can see the meaning of this individualism: the citizen must first fit into a structure and protect himself; he must enter into a social contract with other citizens of his own kind. And it is this smaller community that will confer upon him his individual function and personal worth. Within the association he will take initiatives, will be able to advocate a personal policy and, if he is able to, influence the collective orientation.

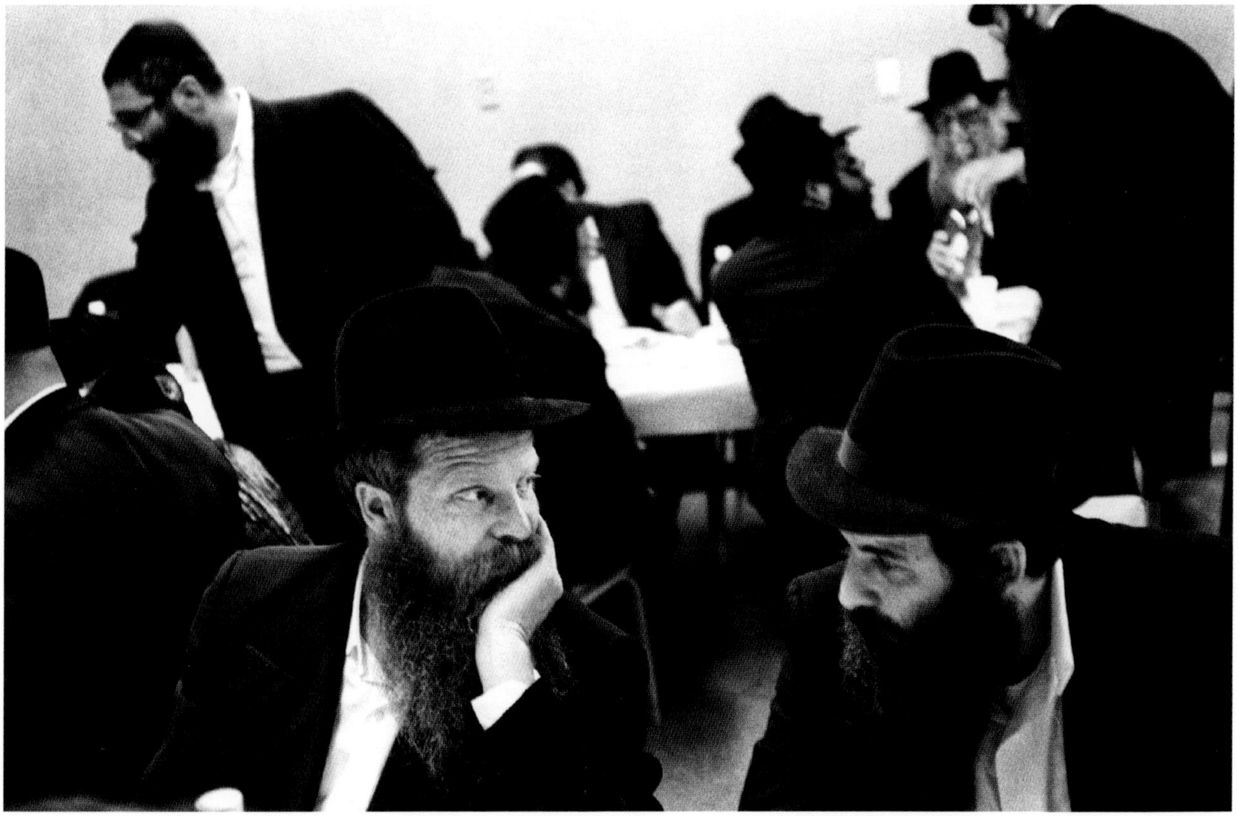

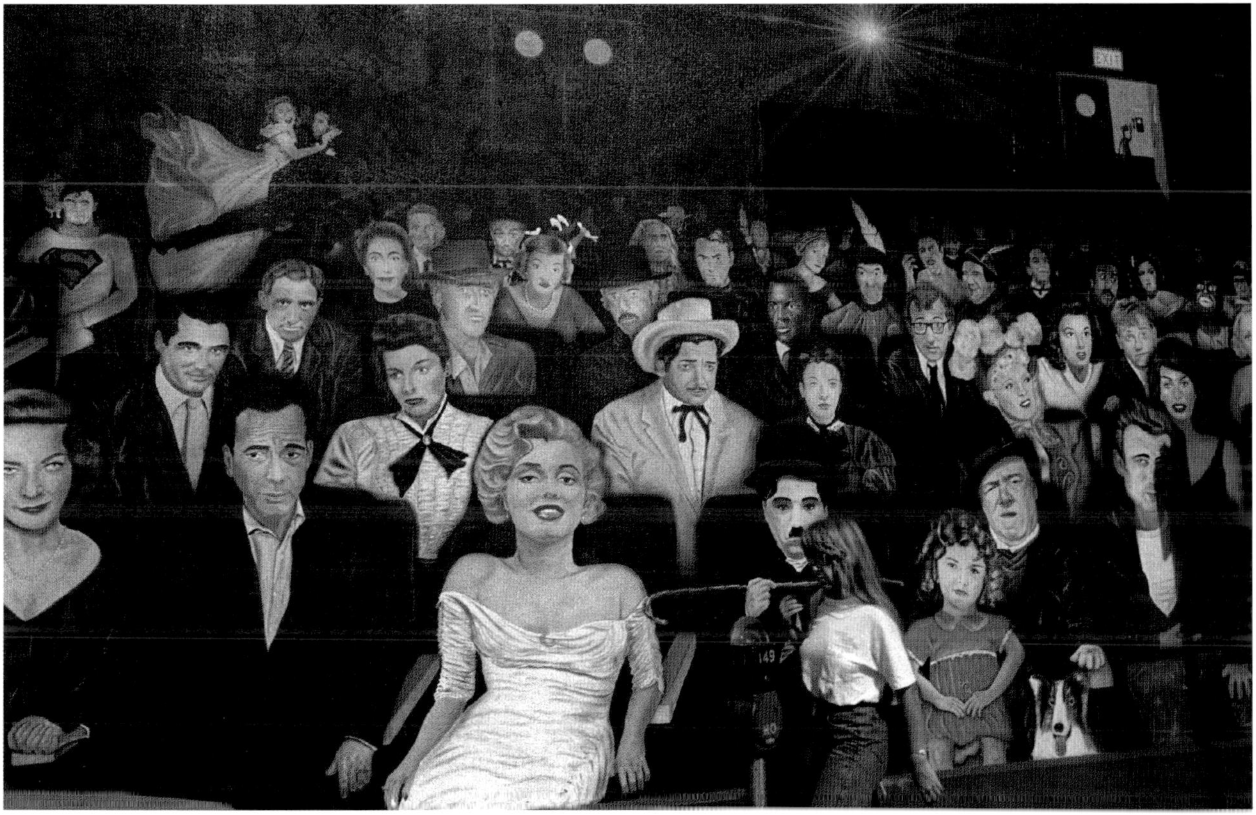
EXIT

Just as the solitary individual arouses distrust in the US, so this directed, hedged-in individualism is encouraged.

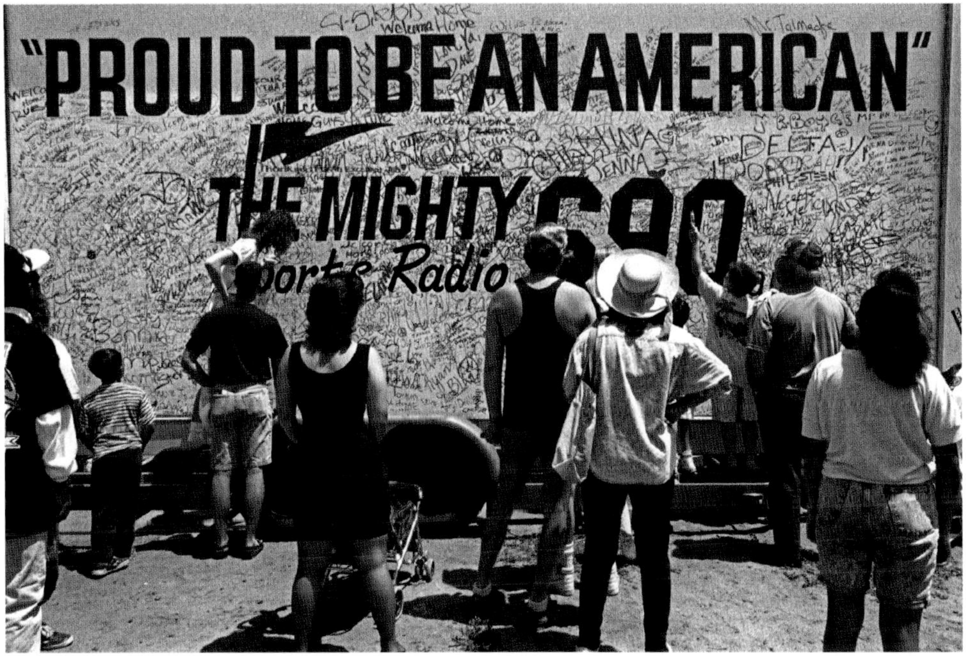
“PROUD TO BE AN AMERICAN”
MIGHTY
Radio

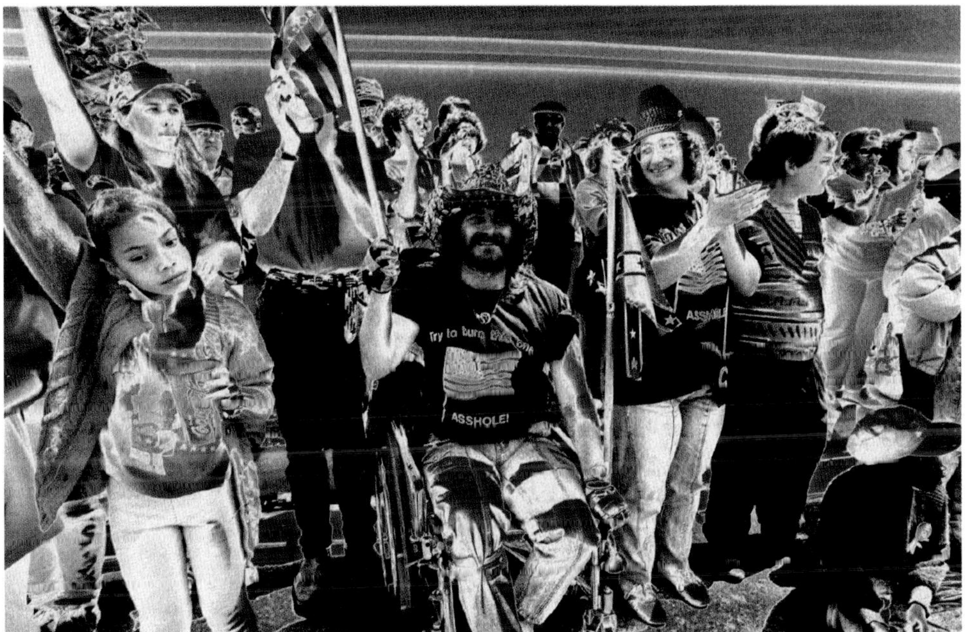
ASSHOLE!

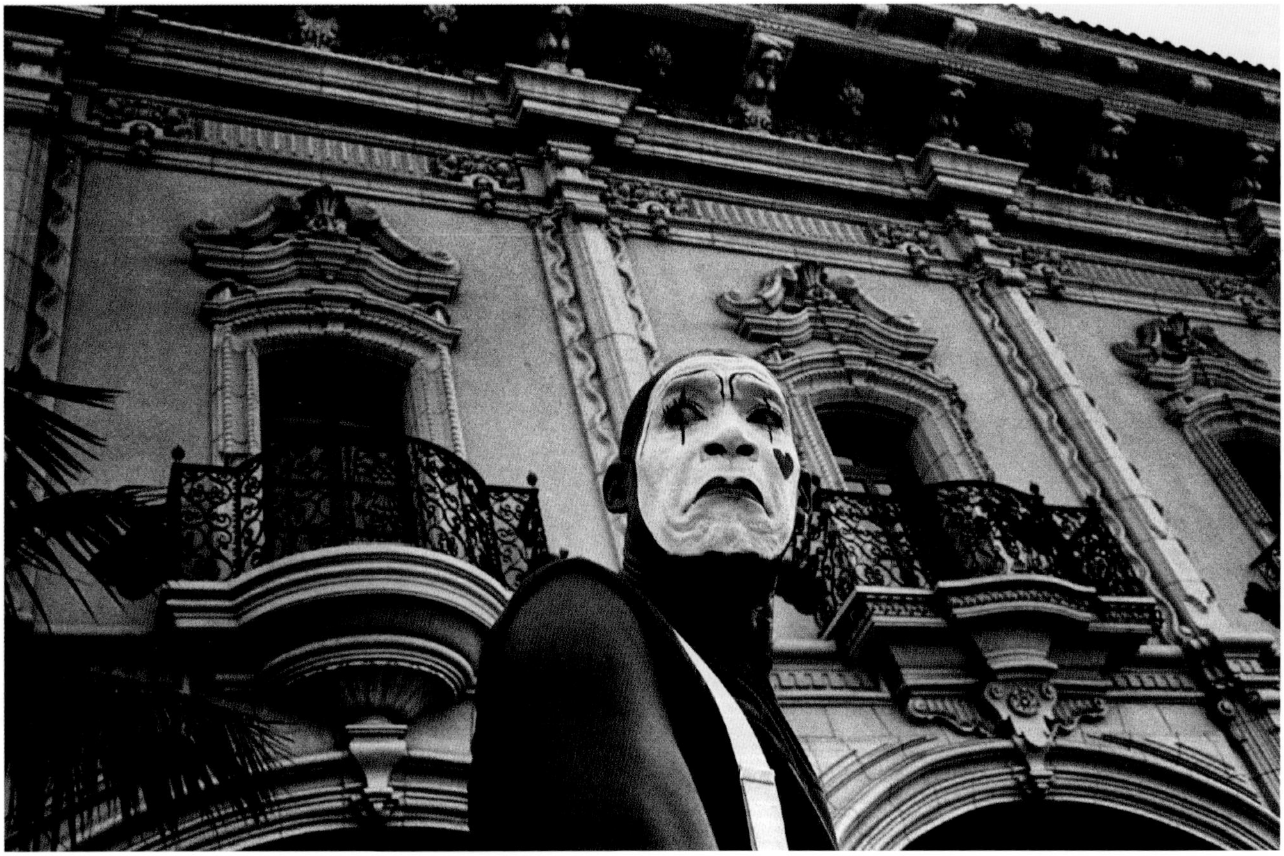

This is illustrated, at quite another level, by the attempts made by leaders of industry to foster self-criticism among their staff.

When the worker is in a trade union, when government and managerial propaganda have sufficiently integrated him into the community, then he is asked to distinguish himself from the others and show initiative. On more than one occasion, at a factory entrance, we came across brightly coloured booths where improvements proposed by members of the workforce were displayed under glass, together with photographs of their inventors who frequently receive bonuses for their efforts.

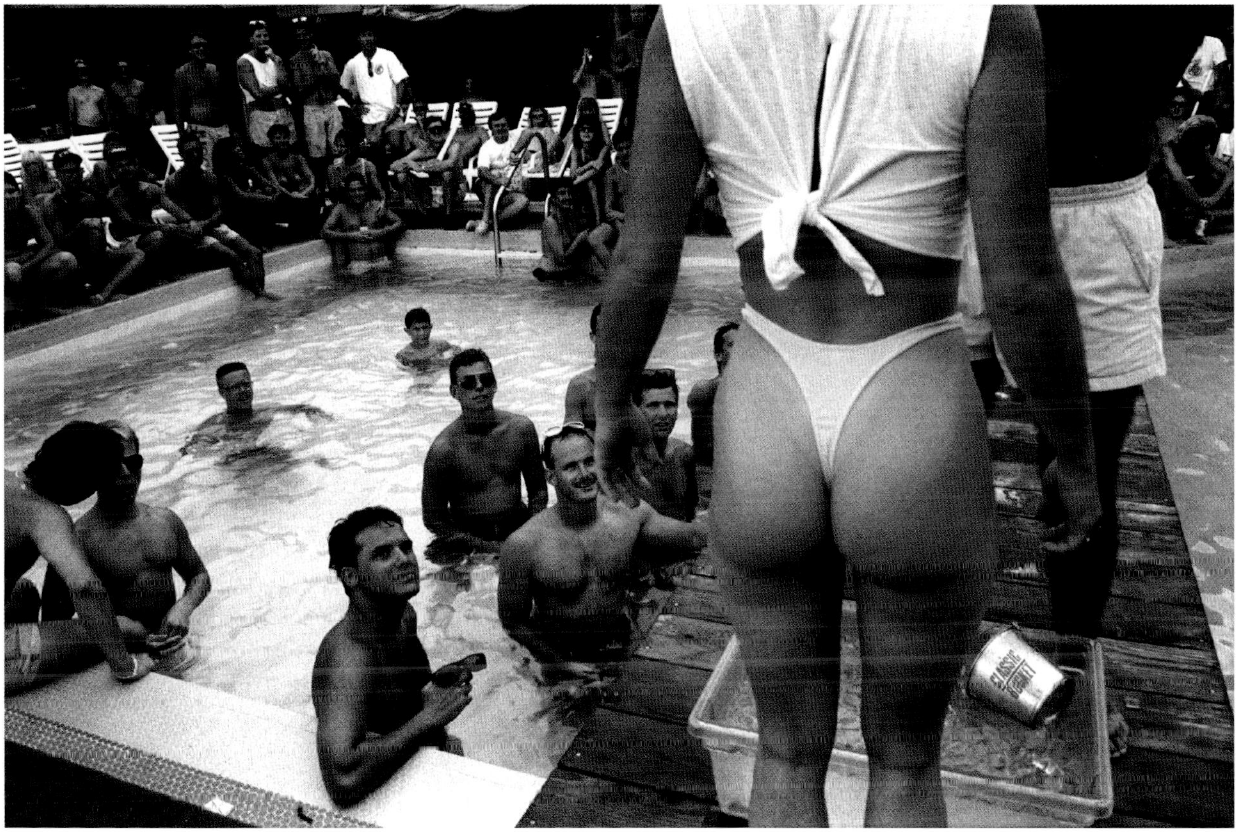

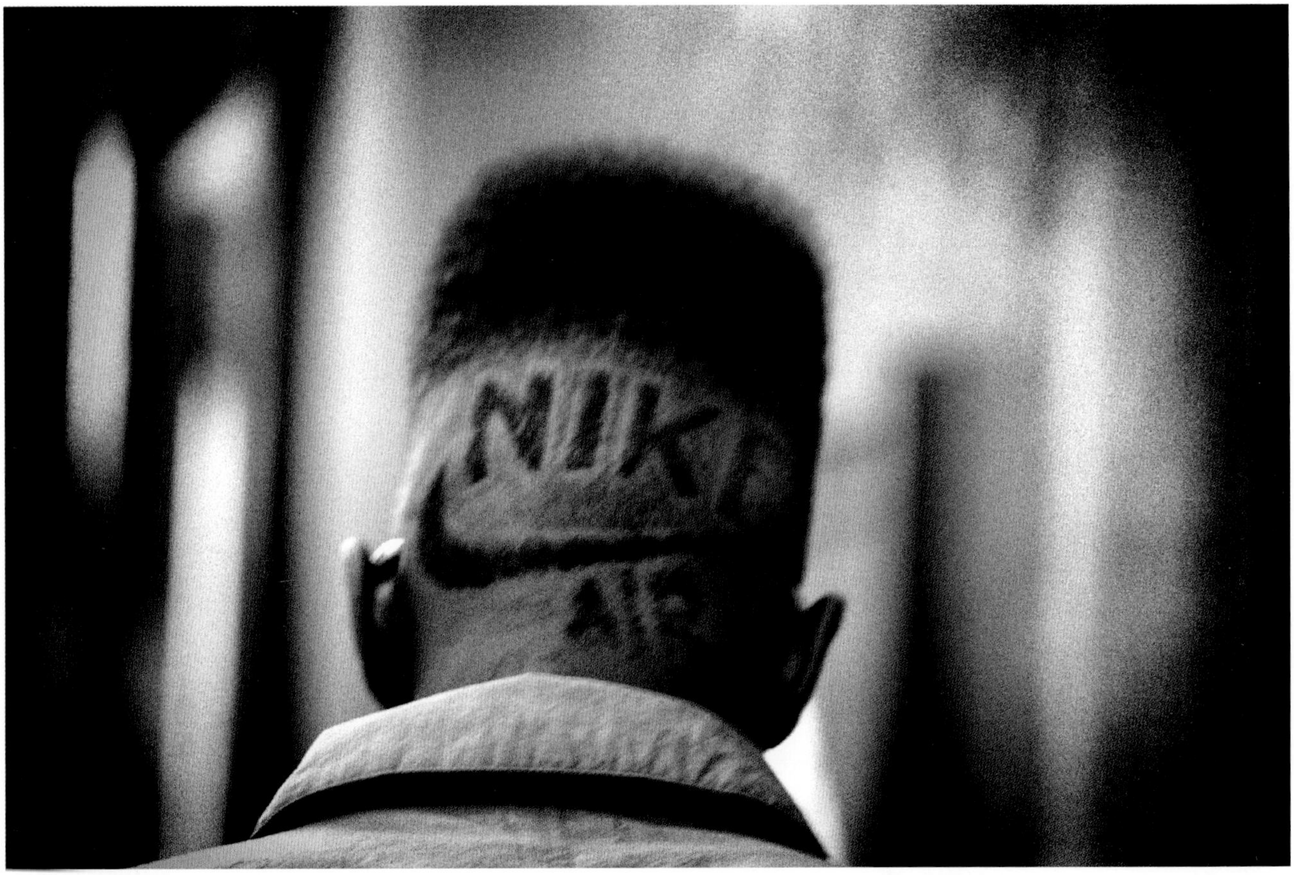

I have said enough, I hope, to convey how the American citizen is subjected, from cradle to grave, to an intense force of organization and Americanization; how he is first depersonalized by a constant appeal to his reason, public-spiritedness and freedom; and how, when he is duly slotted into the nation by professional organizations and by the associations for moral edification and education, he suddenly recovers awareness of himself and his personal autonomy.

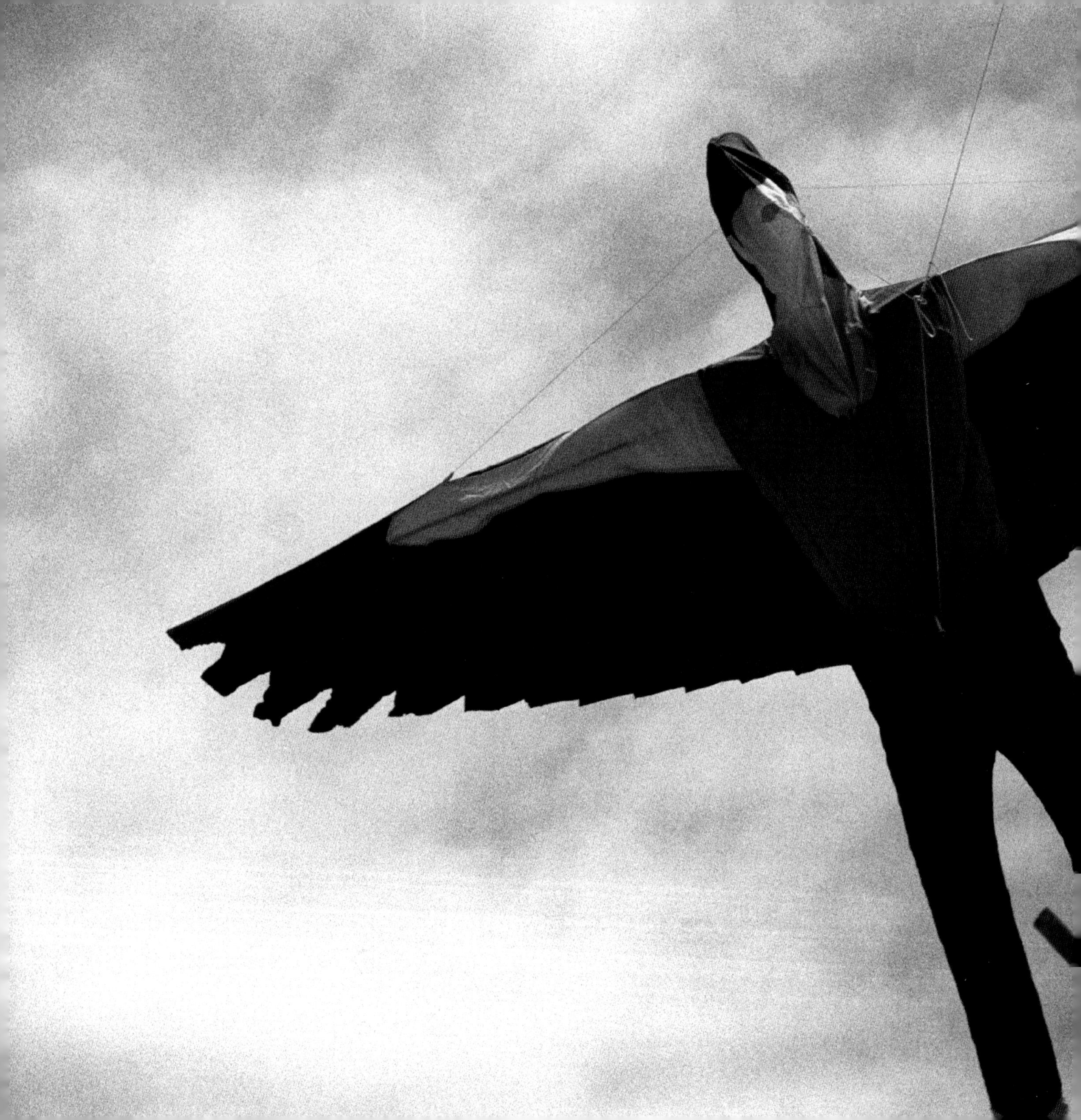

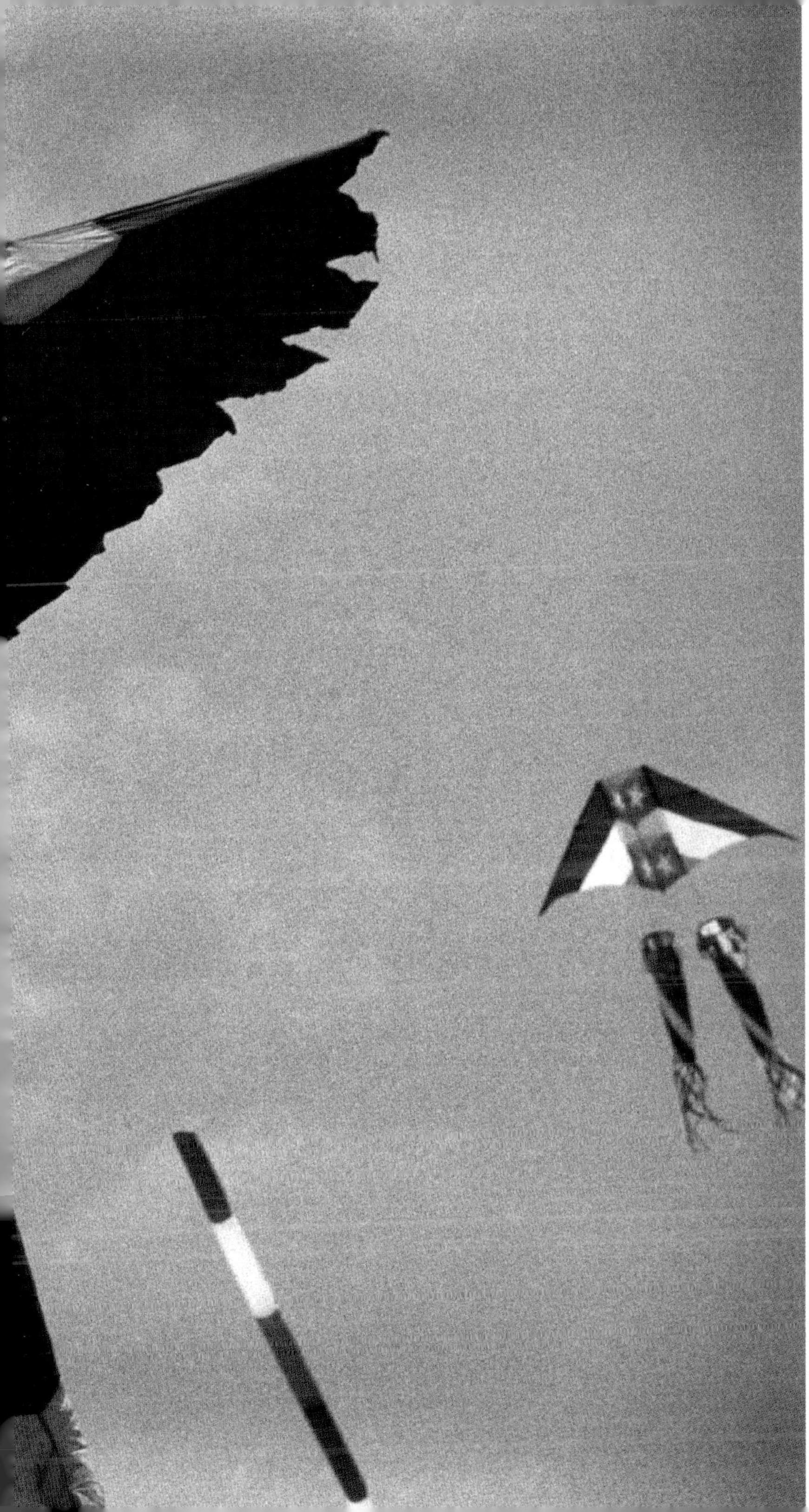

He is then free to escape towards an almost Nietzschean individualism symbolized by the skyscrapers in the clear skies of New York.

In any event, it is not individualism that is the basic element here, but conformism.

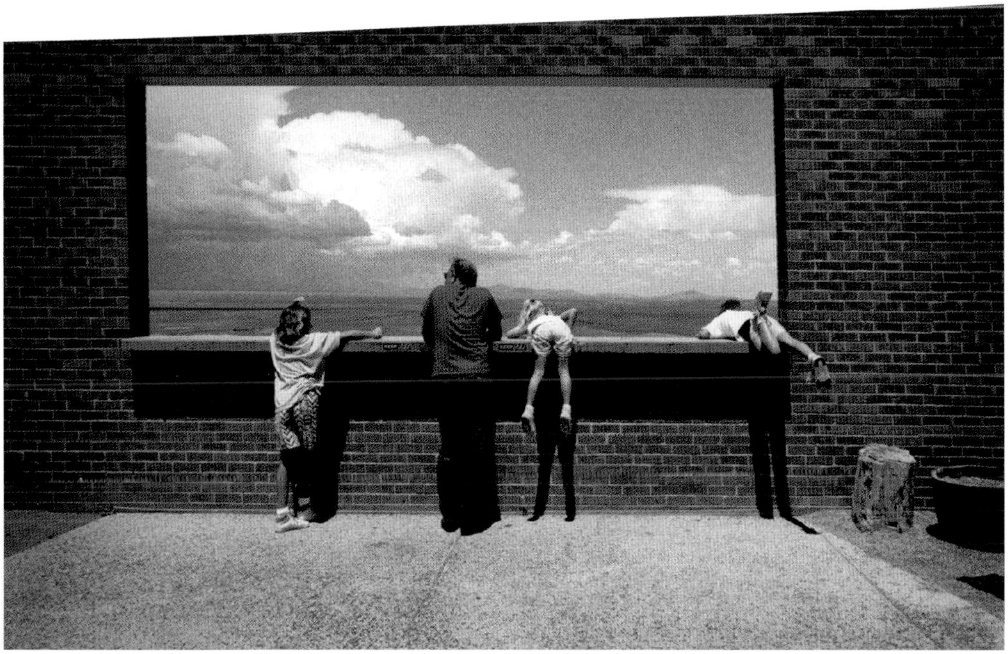

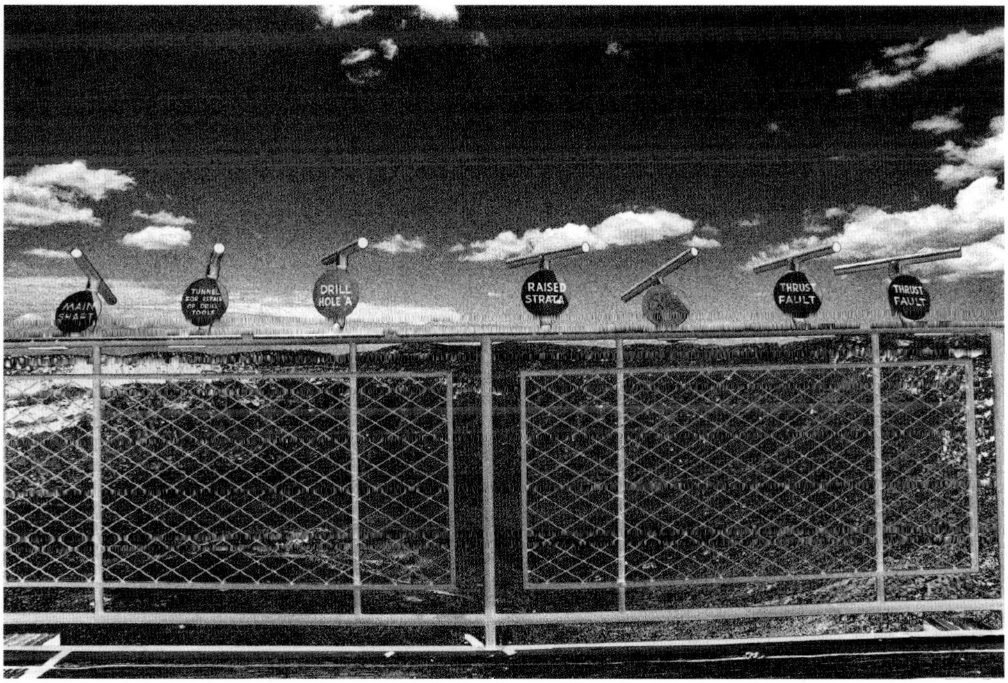
MAIN SHAFT
TUNNEL FOR REPAIR OF DRILL TOOLS
DRILL HOLE A
RAISED STRATA
THRUST FAULT
THRUST FAULT

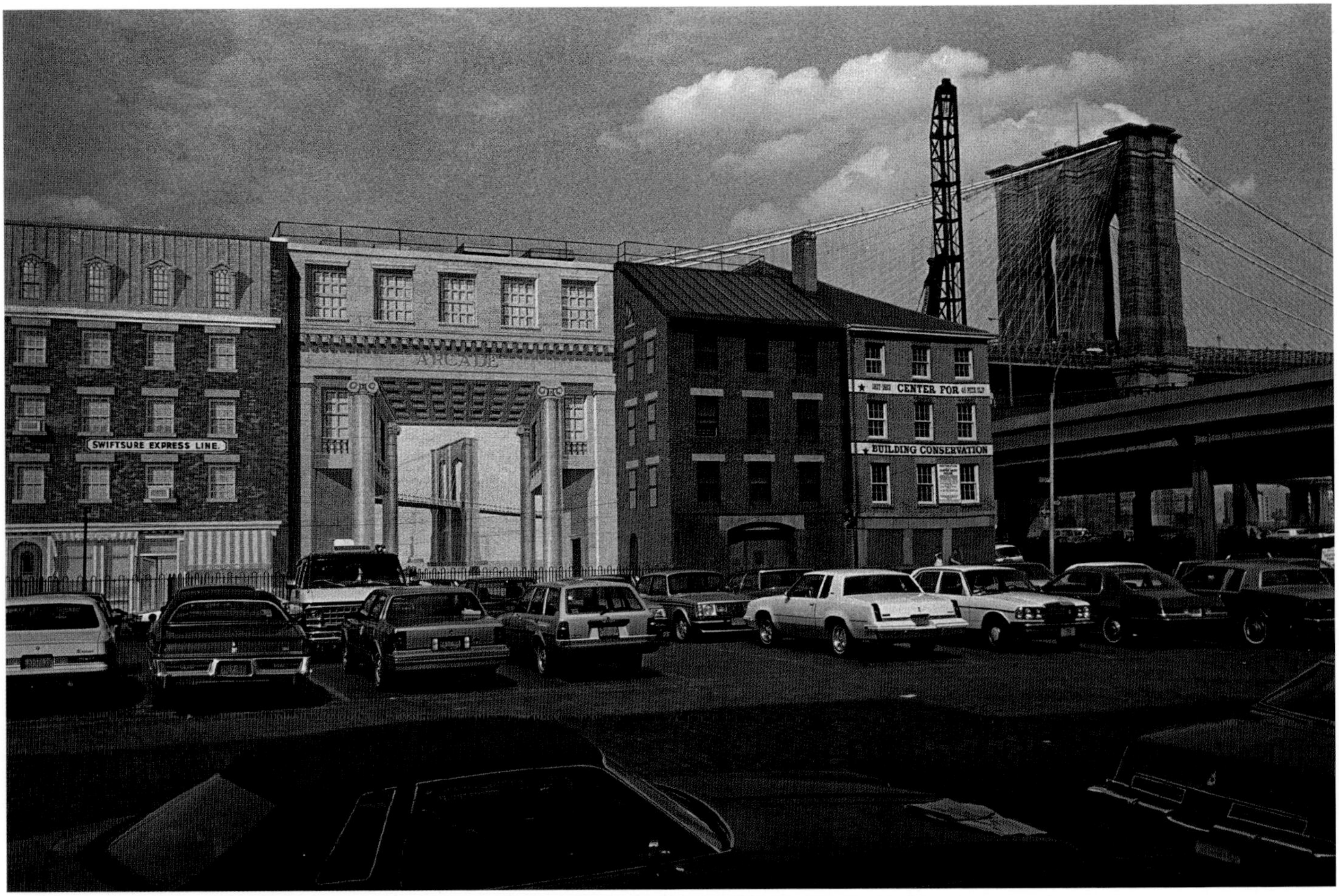
SWIFTSURE EXPRESS LINE.
ARCADE
CENTER FOR
BUILDING CONSERVATION

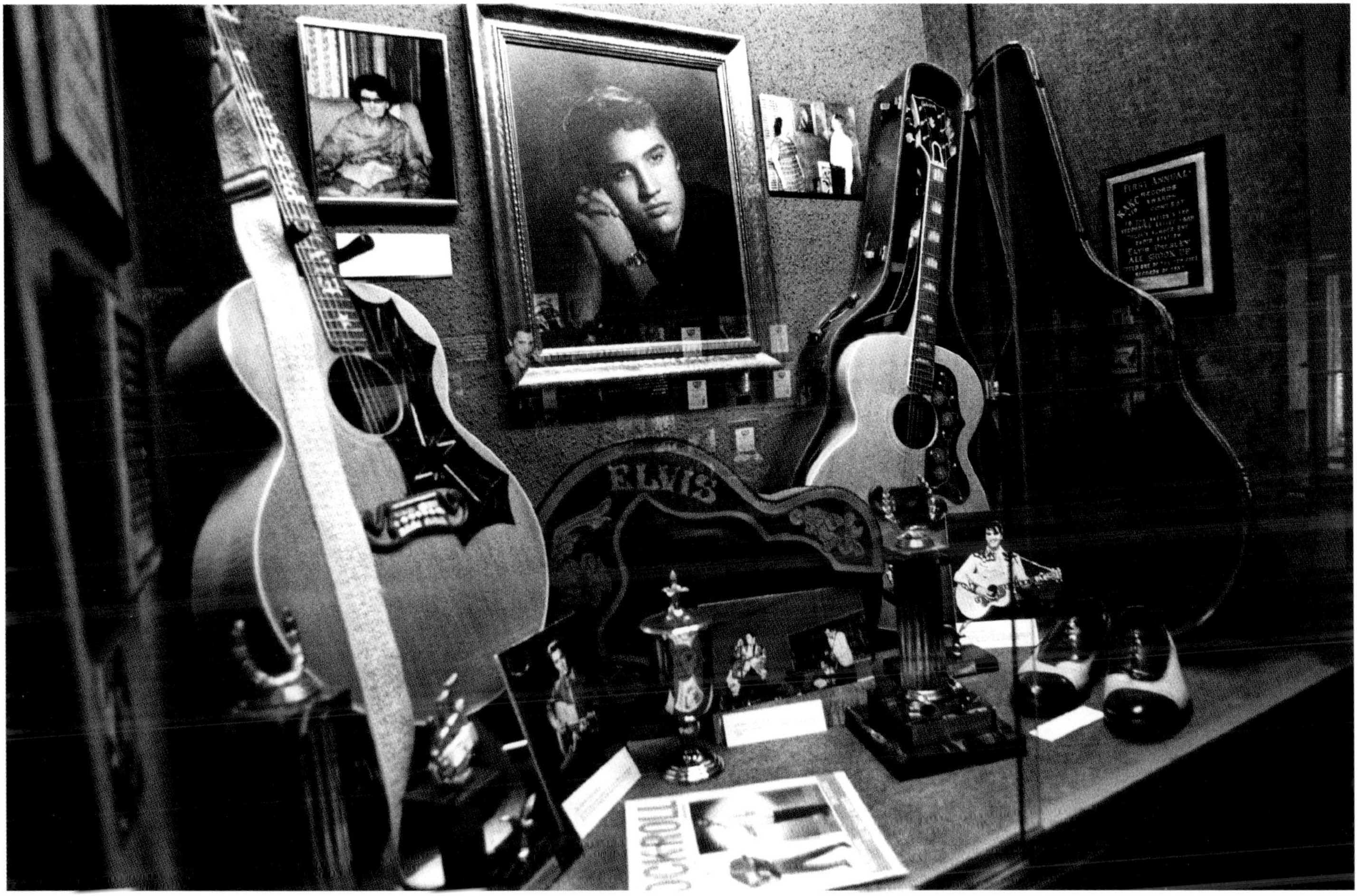
ELVIS

Personality must be won: it is a social function or the affirmation of success.

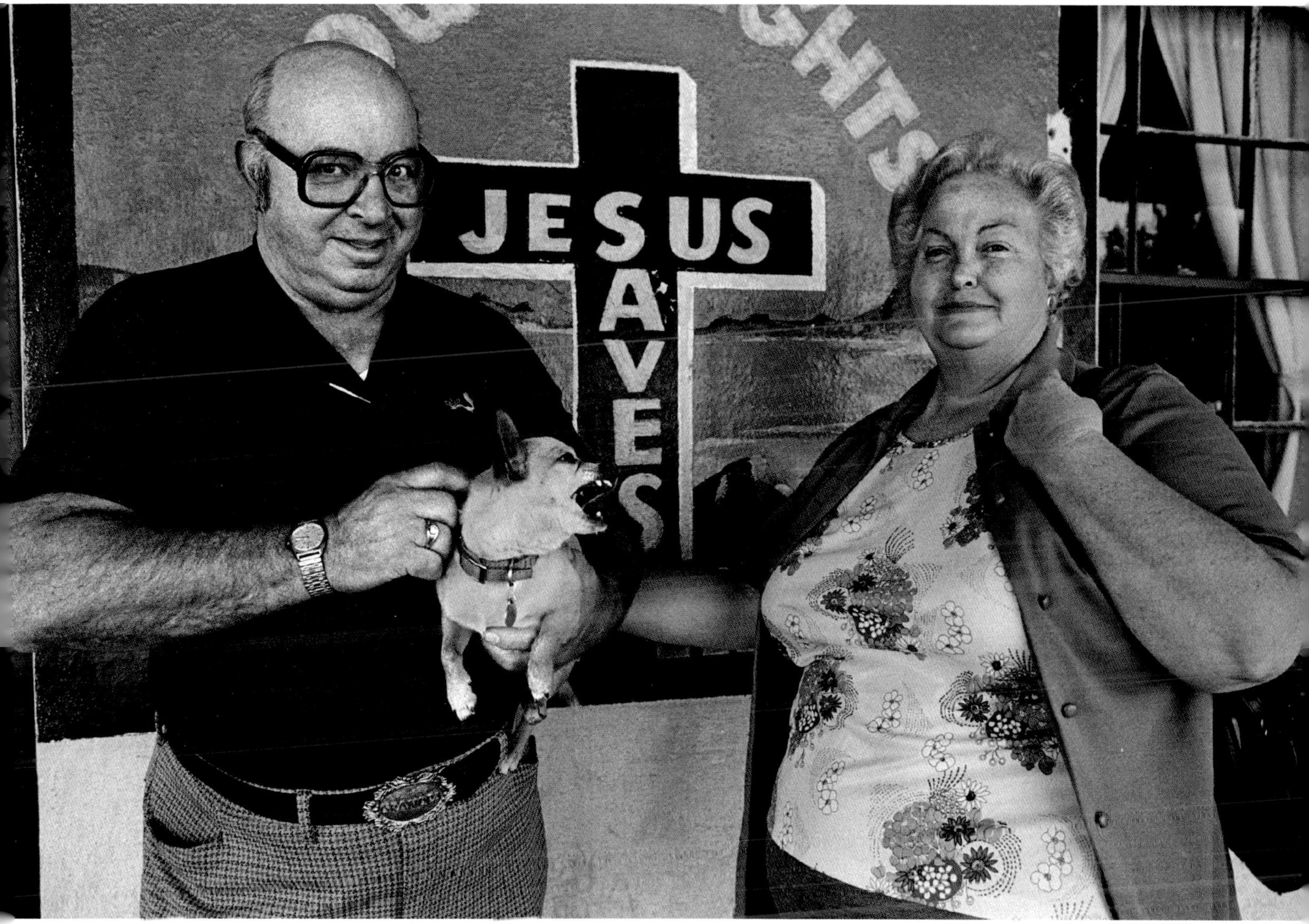
JESUS
SAVES

Photograph captions

PAGE *v*	*American Coffin.* Yosemite, California. 2006
PAGE *vi*	*Storm at the Bridge.* New York, New York. 2011.
PAGE *viii* (*left*)	*Trailer Park.* Yuma, Arizona. 1984.
PAGE *viii* (*right*)	*Urban Transformations.* Dayton, Ohio. 1955.
PAGE 1	*In Memory Of.* Los Angeles, California. 1990.
PAGES 2–3	*An Office Full of Love.* Los Angeles, California. 1988.
PAGE 5	*Emotional Crisis.* Amarillo, Texas. 1993.
PAGE 6	*The Pause on the Road.* Tucson, Arizona. 1985.
PAGE 7	*Defying Gravity.* Anaheim, California. 1990.
PAGE 8 (*above*)	*Bird Worship.* Yuma, Arizona. 1984.
PAGE 8 (*below*)	*We were Already there Before the Americans Arrived.* El Paso, Texas. 1989.
PAGE 11	*Past Times.* Reno, Nevada. 1990.
PAGE 12	*The Red Balloon.* Las Vegas, Nevada. 2001.
PAGE 15 (*above*)	*Happiness Sold Here.* Houston, Texas. 2006.
PAGE 15 (*below, left*)	*In the Era of Oil.* Van Horn, Texas. 1989.
PAGE 15 (*below, right*)	*The Five O'clock News.* Houston, Texas. 1993.

PAGE 16 (*above*)	*Mexican in the Process of Melting*. New York, New York. 1986.
PAGE 16 (*below*)	*Hassidic Boys*. New York, New York. 1986.
PAGE 18	*Four Women in a Subway Car*. New York, New York. 1983.
PAGE 19	*White-Skinned Indian*. Yuma, Arizona. 1986.
PAGE 21	*American Pride*. New York, New York. 1985.
PAGE 22 (*above*)	*La Maja*. Los Angeles, California. 1996.
PAGE 22 (*below*)	*Workers without Borders*. Los Angeles, California. 2006.
PAGE 25 (*above*)	*You're Dead*. San Diego, California. 1988.
PAGE 25 (*below*)	*Have You Attacked America Today*? New York, New York. 1989.
PAGE 26	*Dog Act*. San Francisco, California. 1989.
PAGE 29	*US Tabloids*. Montgomery, Alabama. 1990.
PAGE 30 (*left*)	*The TV Era*. Lake Buena Vista, Florida. 1960.
PAGE 30 (*right*)	*Impersonators*. San Francisco, California. 1988.
PAGE 33	*Meditation*. New York, New York. 1990.
PAGE 34	*Lonely Connoisseur*. New York, New York. 1985.
PAGE 35	*Lonely Coffee Drinker*. Los Angeles, California. 1988.
PAGE 36 (*above*)	*Drugged Wall*. Los Angeles, California. 1988.
PAGE 36 (*below*)	*Latin Rhythms*. New York, New York. 1985.
PAGES 38–9	*Writing on the Wall*. Los Angeles, California. 1989.
PAGES 40–1	*Peep Holes*. New York, New York. 1985.
PAGES 42–3	*A Verb, Not a Noun*. New York, New York. 1985.
PAGE 45 (*left*)	*Shoe Hospital*. Houston, Texas. 2002.
PAGE 45 (*right*)	*Camera Shop*. Los Angeles, California. 1999
PAGE 46	*We Sell for Less*. Montgomery, Alabama. 1990.
PAGE 49	*In the Clouds*. New York, New York. 2010.

PAGE 53 (*left*) *The 'Scape . . .* Los Angeles, California. 1993.

PAGE 53 (*right*) *Levels.* Lake Buena Vista, Florida. 1990.

PAGE 54 (*above*) *Protected Sheep.* Camden, Maine. 1989.

PAGE 54 (*below*) *Obey.* Los Angeles, California. 1988.

PAGE 57 (*above*) *Shooting Gallery.* Montgomery, Alabama. 1990.

PAGE 57 (*below*) *Mexican Migrant Workers.* Riverside, California. 1990.

PAGE 58 *Grandma Guns.* Yuma, Arizona. 1994.

PAGE 61 (*left*) *Pickpocket.* New York, New York. 1985.

PAGE 61 (*right*) *Loveland.* Imperial Valley, California. 1993.

PAGE 63 *Victoria's Secrets.* Los Angeles, California. 2007.

PAGE 64 *Mickey Mouse Family.* Yuma, Arizona. 1985.

PAGE 67 (*left*) *Poster Boy.* Clarkesville, Tennessee. 2006.

PAGE 67 (*right*) *Chests.* Clarkesville, Tennessee. 2006.

PAGE 70 *Techno Boy.* San Diego, California. 2003.

PAGE 73 (*above*) *Trailer with the Toys 1.* El Paso, Texas. 1989.

PAGE 73 (*below*) *Trailer with the Toys 2.* Van Horn, Texas. 1989.

PAGES 74–5 *A Mariachi, in the Park.* Anaheim, California. 1990.

PAGE 76 *Ham and Eggs.* Anaheim, California. 1990.

PAGE 79 *Square Dance.* New York, New York. 1987.

PAGE 83 *The Streets without Name.* New York, New York. 1985.

PAGE 84 *Amusement Gallery.* New York, New York. 1985.

PAGE 87 *The Twin Towers.* New York, New York. 1989.

PAGE 88 *St Patrick's Cathedral.* New York, New York. 1989.

PAGE 91 *A Lost Cloud.* Texas. 1989.

PAGE 92 *Four Palm Trees and a Cannon.* Yuma, Arizona. 1985.

PAGE 95	*Three D.* Riverside, California. 1990.
PAGE 96	*Luxury Furs.* New York, New York. 2006.
PAGES 98–9	*State of Mind.* Washington DC. 1990.
PAGE 101 (*above*)	*Housing Project.* Tucson, Arizona. 1989.
PAGE 101 (*below*)	*Retirement Community.* Miami, Florida. 1990.
PAGE 102 (*left*)	*Going Out of Business 1.* Dayton, Ohio. 1955.
PAGE 102 (*right*)	*Going Out of Business 2.* Dayton, Ohio. 1955.
PAGE 104	*Going Out of Business 3.* Dayton, Ohio. 1955.
PAGE 105	*Going Out of Business 4.* Dayton, Ohio. 1955.
PAGE 107	*Dragonfly.* New York, New York. 1985.
PAGE 108 (*left*)	*The News.* New York, New York. 1985.
PAGE 108 (*right*)	*Schizophrenia.* Los Angeles, California. 1988.
PAGE 111	*Oh, for the Memories.* Los Angeles, California. 1988.
PAGE 112 (*above*)	*Marbellous Ladies.* Washington DC. 1990.
PAGE 112 (*below*)	*In the Senate.* Washington DC. 1990.
PAGE 115	*Ronald in the Sky.* New York, New York. 1990.
PAGE 116	*Chaplin.* Los Angeles, California. 1988.
PAGE 119 (*above*)	*Tea Party.* Los Angeles, California. 1984.
PAGE 119 (*below*)	*Gossip Club.* New York, New York. 1985.
PAGE 120–1	*Multiple Realities.* New York, New York. 1985.
PAGE 122	*Bingo Hall.* Florida. 1990.
PAGE 125	*Carrot Head.* Los Angeles, California. 2002.
PAGE 126	*Girl with Monster.* Los Angeles, California. 1999.
PAGE 128	*Friday Evening.* Los Angeles, California. 1989.
PAGE 129	*Hollywood Boulevard.* Los Angeles, California. 1988.

PAGE 131 (*above*)	*Proud to be an American.* Oceanside, California. 1991.
PAGE 131 (*below*)	*Try Burning This One.* Oceanside, California. 1991.
PAGE 132	*Mime.* San Diego, California. 1988.
PAGE 135	*A Matter of Thongs.* Panama City, Florida. 1990.
PAGE 136	*Nike Head.* Los Angeles, California. 1990.
PAGE 138–9	*The Kites.* Los Angeles, California. 1990.
PAGE 141 (*above*)	*Window on Winslow.* Winslow, Arizona. 1990.
PAGE 141 (*below*)	*Guided Views.* Winslow, Arizona. 1990.
PAGE 142	*Trompe l'oeil.* New York, New York. 1985.
PAGE 143	*Elvis Memorial.* Memphis, Tennessee. 1990.
PAGE 145	*Jesus Saves Here.* Yuma, Arizona. 1984.